Sternwheelers & Canyon Cats

OTHER BOOKS BY JACK BOUDREAU

Crazy Man's Creek
Grizzly Bear Mountain
Mountains, Campfires & Memories
Wilderness Dreams
Wild & Free (with Frank Cooke)

Sternwheelers & Canyon Cats

Whitewater Freighting on the Upper Fraser

Jack Boudreau
with a foreword by Mike Nash

CAITLIN PRESS

Caitlin Press
P.O. Box 219
Madeira Park, BC V0N 2H0
www.harbourpublishing.com

Cover: BC Archives G-03259, SS *Conveyor* in the Fraser River above Prince George (cropped and tinted)
Printed and bound in Canada

Caitlin Press acknowledges financial support from the Government of Canada through the Book Publishing Industry Development Program and the Canada Council for the Arts, and from the Province of British Columbia through the BC Arts Council and the Book Publishing Tax Credit.

THE CANADA COUNCIL | LE CONSEIL DES ARTS
FOR THE ARTS | DU CANADA
SINCE 1957 | DEPUIS 1957

BRITISH
COLUMBIA
ARTS COUNCIL
Supported by the Province of British Columbia

Library and Archives Canada Cataloguing in Publication

Boudreau, Jack, 1933–
    Sternwheelers and canyon cats : whitewater freighting on the upper Fraser / Jack Boudreau.

Includes bibliographical references and index.
ISBN 1-894759-20-6

    1. Paddle steamers—British Columbia—Fraser River—History.
2. Steam-navigation—British Columbia—Fraser River—History. 3. Fraser River (B.C.)—Navigation—History. 4. Inland water transportation—Freight—British Columbia—Fraser River—History. I. Title.

HE635.Z7F73 2006   386'.354097113   C2006-903357-9

This book is dedicated to a courageous group of men called the Canyon Cats, who took up residence at the head of the Grand Canyon of the Fraser River during the years 1911–1913. These men moved scows, rafts and boats through the rapids and whirlpools for inexperienced river travellers who could afford their services. It was hazardous work—in one instance, four of five Cats were drowned when their scow hit Green's Rock. The surviving Cat immediately went back to the head of the canyon and brought another scow through. Though they made the equivalent of fifty thousand dollars per month, many never lived long enough to spend their earnings.

Green's Rock in low water, 1911.

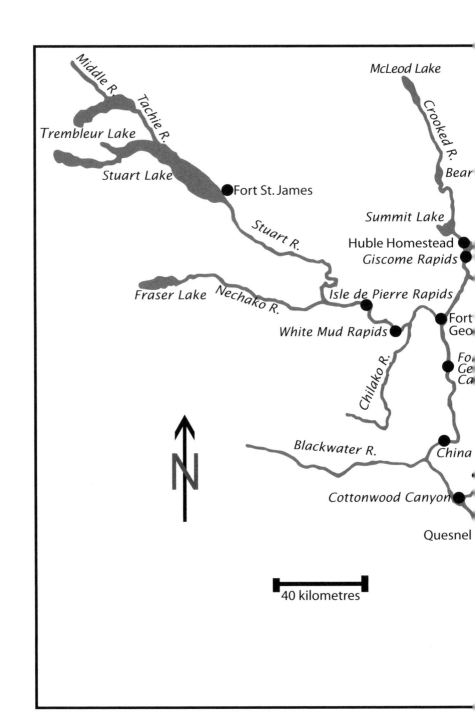

NAVIGATION ON THE UPPER FRASER RIVER

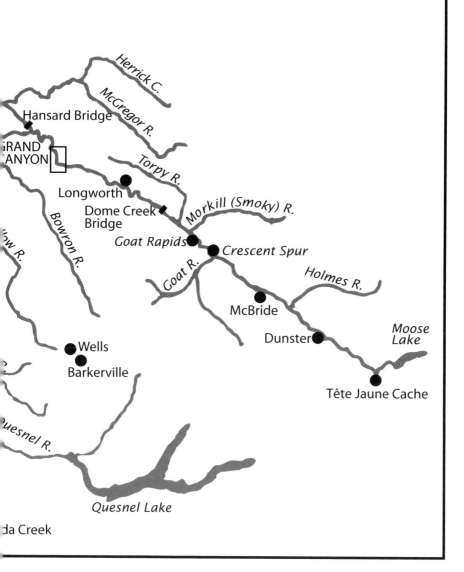

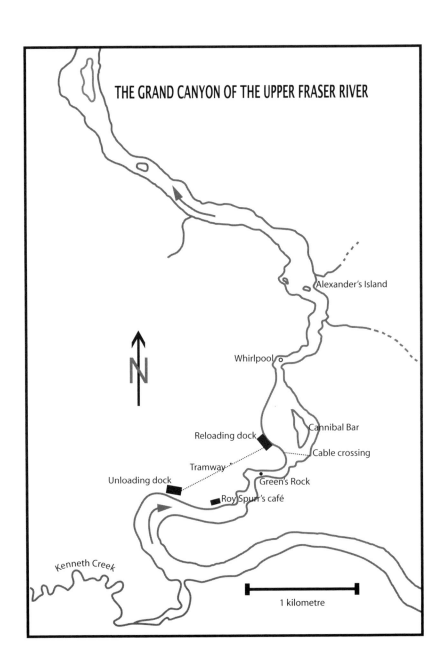

THE GRAND CANYON OF THE UPPER FRASER RIVER

Alexander's Island

N

Whirlpool

Cannibal Bar

Reloading dock

Cable crossing

Tramway

Unloading dock

Green's Rock

Roy Spurr's café

Kenneth Creek

1 kilometre

Contents

Acknowledgements

First I wish to thank all of the newspapers, books, magazines and historical quarterlies that I have so frequently quoted. I am mindful of the fact that had these thoughtful people not put pen to paper there would be little or no historical notes to quote from.

Once again I must thank the staff of the Bob Harkins Branch of the Prince George Public Library for their endless assistance; as well, a special thanks to the libraries of the College of New Caledonia and the University of Northern British Columbia.

To Mike Nash, many thanks for contributing the foreword to this book, and for your assistance with the maps.

To James Tirrul-Jones and the Huble Homestead/Giscome Portage Historical Society, for pictures and information concerning the Giscome Portage, I extend many thanks.

Others who assisted in one way or another were Melanie Cummins, Olive Williams, Kathy Plett, Louisa Mueller, Elizabeth and Dale Sinclair, Eleanor and Bob Dondale, Ramona Rose, Shirley and Paul Richter, Jean and Charlie Benton, Maxine and Peter Koppe, Edna and Val Roth, Elarry Evasin, Gus Lund, Kent Sedgwick, Ben

Meisner, Fred Spurr, Roy Groeneveld, Steve and Brian Marynovich, Vern Gogolin, Gerald Flynn, Eric Klaubauf and Steve Buba. As well, I offer a belated thanks to Rick Roos and Mike Murtha, formerly of BC Parks, without whose assistance this book may never have materialized.

I also offer a special thanks to Kevin Fitzsimmons, Brent Gobbi and Peter Koppe for their assistance in the filming of the documentary about the Grand Canyon of the Fraser River.

A final point I must make concerns the many quotations from newspapers and books that I have used in this book. The reader may justifiably question the veracity of my material because many of the events, such as acts of courage unknown in today's world, border on the impossible. However, much of the quoted information can be checked and the source is as close as the nearest public library.

Enjoy.

—JACK BOUDREAU

Foreword

Mike Nash

Countless lives have been lost navigating unknown rivers in this mountainous land of British Columbia. The number of people drowned throughout the years will never be known, as so many people were travelling alone and no one knew their whereabouts. Jack Boudreau has estimated that at least two hundred people perished in the Grand Canyon of the upper Fraser River, and he thinks it is entirely possible that this is a conservative number.

This canyon is situated 106 miles (170 km) upstream from Prince George (formerly Fort George) and 209 miles (336 km) downstream from Tête Jaune Cache, the head of navigation on the upper Fraser River. River traffic beyond this point was impossible because a huge logjam fifteen metres high blocked the entire river during the years of construction.

This magnificent canyon, with its astounding history, lies in the middle of one of the earth's great strike-slip faults, where large pieces of the planet's ancient crust collided and slid laterally for many hundreds of miles. Known in BC as the Rocky Mountain Trench, it stretches northwest from Tête Jaune to the Yukon Territories, where it continues as the Tintina Trench. The Rocky Mountain Trench also continues southeast from Tête Jaune to the US border, but its origins in the southern part of the province are more obscure.

After countless generations of use by Native North Americans, the first documented activity along the upper river by non-Natives appears to have begun in 1825 and lasted until 1831. During that period, leather was moved from Saskatchewan through the Yellowhead Pass and down the Fraser River to supply the interior of BC, where there was a shortage of big-game animals and consequently a shortage of hides and leather.

The next flurry of activity occurred in 1862, when a party of gold-seekers called the Overlanders made their way across Canada to the Fraser River, where they split into two groups. One group followed the North Thompson River, while the other group followed the Fraser through a treacherous stretch of water in the Grand Canyon. Several of the party that chose this route were lost while attempting to move their rafts and canoes through this dangerous canyon downriver to the goldfields of Barkerville and the lower Fraser River. Their trek was one of starvation, hardship and often death.

In 1972, producer/director Don Eccleston made the film *The Overlanders* based on the incredible journey these people had made over a century earlier. The portion of the movie that Jack Boudreau worked on started with the construction of two large rafts about 70 miles (113 km) upriver from the Grand Canyon. These two rafts—the *Knox* and the *Golden Fleece*—were decked out in a realistic manner, with sleeping quarters and fireplaces on board because of the desire of the Overlanders' crews not to have to pull into shore to cook food.

Jack was one of six riverboat operators hired to move the cast and all their equipment to and from the different locations along the river, as well as to move the rafts and keep them off the bars and shallows. He was surprised at the effort required to make the movie and the great amount of time that was sometimes spent acquiring just a few feet of film.

The portion that Jack worked on was completed at the Grand Canyon before the cast moved on to Quesnel and Barkerville, where the remainder of the film was finished. Jack says that he thoroughly enjoyed the time spent with the film crew. It made him realize that there is much more to making a movie than he had ever imagined. He also gained a great deal of respect for the river when his outboard engine failed right at the entrance to the canyon. Thanks to the quick action taken by riverman Glen Hooker, he was towed to safety just in the nick of time.

Throughout the years a total of twelve sternwheelers ran sections of the upper Fraser River between Tête Jaune and Soda Creek, a distance of 475 miles (765 km). During that time the river took an incredible toll in lives and property, with the Fort George (Red Rock) Canyon 15 miles (24 km) downstream from Prince George posing the greatest threat to these pioneering vessels.

The Grand Canyon, however, was by far the most dangerous for scows, rafts and canoes. Much respected by the Native North Americans, this canyon lay silently remote from the outside world and, in the words of Jack Boudreau, seemingly ". . . a monster-in-waiting, hungry for the feast of victims it would eventually devour."

During the construction of the Grand Trunk Pacific Railway (GTP)—1906 to 1914—this canyon was the chief obstacle to river traffic. It was a place of urgent activity during the navigation season, and was the scene of many remarkable events and more than its share of tragedies. During that period a great many loaded scows were moved upriver to supply the surveyors laying out the new grade for the GTP Railway. After 1911, the railhead reached Tête Jaune from the east and an enormous number of rafts, scows and canoes brought people, supplies and contractors downriver. Perhaps the best known of these scow pilots was George Williams, affectionately called the "Wizard of the River" by his peers. Williams was undoubtedly one of the best whitewater men on the mighty Fraser, and he proved it by successfully moving thousands of tons of freight through the rapids and canyons.

From 1909 to 1913, several sternwheelers hauled people and freight along the upper waterway. Following the completion of the railway, the big steamboats were no longer able to access the upper river because—contrary to navigation regulations, which forbade blocking a navigable stream—the GTP Railway had constructed low-level bridges across the river. The steamboat companies fought the railroad in the courts for years, but eventually their damage claim for $75,000 was dismissed. The result of this was that, aside from freight shipped to Giscome Portage, the GTP Railway was the sole distributor of freight along the upper river from 1914 on. Barred from the upper river, the steamers were then limited to travelling downstream between Prince George and Soda Creek.

After a period of quiet along the upper river, several logging companies moved logs through the canyon to their sawmills, but these river drives, as they were called, were discontinued in the 1960s. Since then, very little activity has taken place in this mighty canyon, and another period of quiet has returned.

Throughout the busy years, the Grand Canyon claimed hundreds of lives. With Green's Rock in the upper rapids and the whirlpool in the lower rapids, the loss of lives and goods was almost beyond belief. Many of these tragedies and adventures are told in the following stories, where courage, sacrifice and tragedy were the order of the day.

About a dozen brave men called Canyon Cats were stationed at the head of the Grand Canyon. These men moved scows, boats and rafts through the perilous water for a hefty price. Some of them did not live long enough to spend their substantial earnings.

Between 1908 and 1914 several powdermen helped clear the river by blasting the most dangerous rocks, reefs and logjams to make safer passage for the scows and steamers. Frank Freeman was foremost among these blasters; he was instrumental in blasting at the Grand Canyon, the Isle de Pierre Rapids, the White Mud (Sestino) Rapids, the Goat River Rapids, the Giscome Rapids and, in 1914, the Soda Creek Rapids.

In the late 1980s, Joe Plenk of Prince George took an interest in the Grand Canyon and began clearing trails there. Following his lead, in the spring of 1991, I made the first of many treks into the Grand Canyon. Later that year I sent a proposal to the Ministry of Forests for the Grand Canyon to be designated a recreation site, but it was turned down. In June 1992 I prepared a report for BC Parks titled "Proposal: Grand Canyon Provincial Park." As a result of this proposal, BC Parks placed a reserve on the Grand Canyon and later in the 1990s the Prince George Land and Resource Management Plan (LRMP) recommended its protection. The LRMP was approved in March 1999 and the Grand Canyon became part of the Sugarbowl–Grizzly Den Provincial Park in June 2000.

Jack Boudreau grew up just twenty-five miles (40 km) upriver from the Grand Canyon in the small railway and river community of Penny. During his early life in the Rocky Mountain Trench, Jack heard many interesting stories firsthand from pioneers of the area. He had the foresight to write a lot of the information down and to add to it during his years with the BC Forest Service. After he took early retirement from the Forest Service, Jack put much of this information together for his first book, *Crazy Man's Creek*, set in the river valleys and mountains around Penny. Published in 1998 by Caitlin Press, it immediately hit the BC Bestseller List, where it stayed number one for over four months. Two years later he followed it with another bestseller, *Grizzly Bear Mountain*, which, like Jack's first book, was set above the Grand Canyon. So it was natural when the Grand Canyon became a provincial park for BC Parks to ask Jack Boudreau to re-search and document the canyon. The ten-thousand-word paper he produced gave me new insights into the history of the canyon, and soon after reading it I suggested to him that he should write a book about it. After a couple of years of prodding, by which time he had produced three more books, he finally told me that this story of the rivers and canyons of the area would be his next project. This book is a timely addition to the history and literature of the interior of BC. It will, I hope, give you the same enjoyment that I have had as you learn about this long-neglected piece of British Columbia's history.

The most experienced riverman to travel the canyon in the modern era was Ray Mueller of Sinclair Mills, whose home was lo-cated just thirteen kilometres downriver from the canyon. Ray fre-quently passed through the canyon in his work as a riverman, trapper and guide. In the fall of 1992 I asked Ray, then eighty-seven years old, to take me through the Grand Canyon in his riverboat. During our journey he talked about the canyon's history and his experiences working its rugged waters since 1925.

Perhaps his most frightening experience occurred the day he was taking his family through the canyon when suddenly a large log shot out of the centre of the eddy. Fortunately, it fell away from his boat rather than onto it.

After guiding many summer walks and a few winter ski trips there, I took another riverboat trip to the canyon in the fall of 2003, when Bob Dondale of Prince George offered Jack Boudreau the services of his riverboat. Along with Bob, Jack and photographer Melanie Cummins, I spent a satisfying day looking over the canyon and studying artifacts such as a steel pin that had been placed in the rock of the upper rapids nearly a century earlier. This pin was used to winch boats and scows upriver and lower them downriver through the rapids.

The reason for the trip was Jack's desire to ascertain the exact position of the infamous Green's Rock—blown away by powdermen—which had been responsible for so many deaths during the railway construction. Not only was his mission successful, he has since discovered a picture of Green's Rock taken in 1911.

One cannot visit this site, two and a half miles (4 km) north of Highway 16, without gaining a sense of what life must have been

Mike Nash and Jack Boudreau at the head of the Grand Canyon, 2003. Courtesy Melanie Cummins

like passing through the canyon during the days of the great river-boats or building the GTP Railway, which closely followed the Fraser River. Sitting on a grassy ledge above the lower canyon, the site of the famous whirlpool, one can visualize the crew of the mighty stern-wheeler *BC Express* struggling to save the ship after a tree jammed its steering mechanism at a critical moment. And one can almost see the diamond salesman running across her deck and leaping in panic to clutch the rock cliff, where he hung in desperation until he was rescued several hours later.

Read on then, if you have the nerve, and try to visualize the enormous challenges and sacrifices made by these pioneers.

Mike Nash is a Prince George writer, outdoorsman, newspaper columnist and magazine contributor, and is the author of the 2004 book *Exploring Prince George: A Guide to North Central BC Outdoors.*

The $\mathbf{1}$eorges

$\mathbf{B}$efore the arrival of the steamers and stagecoaches, Fort George was isolated from the outside world. Fort George Natives, under the direction of Hudson's Bay Company employee Claude Foot and later Charles Bird, did their part to get supplies to the Hudson's Bay post at Fort George. Jimmy Bird did the same for the Hudson's Bay Company in Fort St. James, bringing a few scow-loads of supplies upriver each year. It was a near-impossible task, fighting their way against the river current with five tons of supplies on board, but the twelve to fourteen men employed on the scows always got through to Fort George in about two weeks. Bringing a loaded scow upriver from Quesnel involved unremitting labour. Often this meant using lines to pull the scow in areas where men could walk along the riverbank. In other spots they pushed with poles, or pulled their scow along by hanging onto brush protruding from the shore. All the supplies had to be portaged around the canyons and rapids along the ninety-three-mile (150 km) trip. Because of high water levels, one trip took nineteen days and all the men were exhausted by the time they arrived at Fort George.

In an interview with the *Prince George Citizen* Charles Bird reminisced:

My grandfather was in charge of the store [Hudson's Bay] and I used to work for them occasionally. At that time [1890s] there was just the trading post with the Bird family on one

In areas of deep snowfall caches were placed three to four metres above the ground. Courtesy Prince George Public Library

side and the Indian Reserve on the other, and that meant trapping in the winter for fresh meat, drying meat caught in the summer and smoking fish. My grandmother used to put a fence in the river with a kind of sluice leading to a box. Once the fish got through the fence, they couldn't get out, so they jumped into the sluice and then into the box.

Charles Bird's father owned 160 acres, known as Birdland at the time, between the Hudson's Bay post and the slough. Charles Bird was in charge of the scow trips to and from Quesnel, and recalled that each man received about twenty dollars for the round trip. In the wintertime the food and supplies were brought from Quesnel on pack horses along the narrow foot trail that meandered through the forest.

Jimmy Bird was also an expert riverman in the employ of the Hudson's Bay Company at Fort St. James. He helped move loaded scows from Quesnel to the fort on Stuart Lake. Again, this was a mission bordering on the impossible, and it rightfully won these men a great deal of respect from their peers. I was unable to find out the time required to move the loaded scows from Quesnel to Fort St. James, but I hazard a guess of about one month.

Another view of those days was presented in an interview with the *Fort George Weekly Tribune* on May 22, 1915, when pioneer C.W. Moore recalled:

When I walked from Quesnel to Fort George in 1907, it took me eight days. There were no roads then, but just a trail. I came in with two Indian mail carriers and their dog teams [along with famed surveyor Luther Collins Gunn]. In those days there was only one mail a month—no magazines or newspapers were carried—and any stray ones that we found were treasured accordingly. You may be sure we did not light the fire with any of them.

I remember that first winter when I watched a cache for the Grand Trunk Pacific Railway (GTP) at Point of Rocks, this side of the Willow River. For days at a time I never saw a person. One of my few companions was a blue jay that greeted me every mealtime and eagerly ate what crumbs I could spare.

That bird and the flying squirrels that tried to drop from the trees onto the sugar-cured hams in the cache—which they dearly loved—were about my only friends.

One day there came by two survey parties with, perhaps, twenty men in each, and four sleighs, each drawn by four dogs and driven by Indians. They took supplies from my cache, carrying them on to the next camping place. That was a day to be remembered, for besides the human company, which I welcomed, there were several newspapers left behind. I read those papers through, ads and all, many times that winter. One of the picturesque sights of those days was an occasional dog team that passed loaded with supplies for the surveyors. Those toboggans slipping and sliding easily over the snow with their four-hundred-pound load—one hundred pounds for each dog—were welcome sights. In the summertime the GTP Railroad pack trains of from fifteen to twenty horses took the place of the winter dog teams.

Mr. Moore then went on to describe a typical cache:

Caches such as the one I looked after that winter were more common by far than houses. They were usually built of logs resting on stumps some seven feet above the ground and were about ten feet square and six feet high [3 x 2 m]. Tin was put around the foundation stumps to prevent mice or bush rats from climbing up and eating the food.

Before 1910, the Native mail carriers were often the only means of getting mail through from Quesnel. In fact, a noted Native riverman named Billy Seymour won mention in *Ripley's Believe It or Not* for walking to Quesnel and back to Fort George on snowshoes in a time of forty-two hours. This was a distance of 192 miles (309 km), and his feat provided a perfect example of the inherent endurance often noted among people who live close to nature.

The feeling of remoteness in the Fort George area was lifted somewhat in 1908 when the steamer *Charlotte* nosed into the riverbank at what would soon be known as Steamboat Landing. The next year the steamer *Nechacco* came upriver and landed at the same place, bringing hope that the days of isolation were finally over. South Fort George quickly sprang up around the landing and was for several years the centre of activity in the area.

The downside of the arrival of the steamers was that at most they were only able to run four to six months of the year, leaving six to

Billy Seymour's winter trek from *Ripley's Believe It or Not,* 1908. COURTESY CARIBOO OBSERVER, QUESNEL

eight months without word from the outside except by telegraph, when it was operational, or when Natives brought in the mail from Quesnel.

Soon another townsite sprang up along the Nechako River, which was jokingly referred to as "The Migratory Bird," because it just couldn't stay still. One day it was known as Fort George and the next day it was called Central Fort George. Soon the Hudson's Bay Company got into the act, accusing the townsite of stealing their name. This was true, because the fort area was originally named Fort George when it was started in 1807 by Simon Fraser on one of his trips down the river that still bears his name.

After the arrival of the railroad, the newly purchased Indian Reserve was called Prince George. Understandably this caused confusion among outsiders as to what George the townspeople wanted to be! Some of the outside media jokingly referred to this area as "the Georges" for several years, until the name Prince George gained supremacy.

There was a bit of perverse humour in the area acquiring the name Prince George, because after years of insults and fighting, including court action, both of the original Georges lost out. Their businesses deserted them and set up shop in Prince George. Part of the downfall

A Stage

carrying His Majesty's and other mails, passengers and express, will leave

Fort George for Quesnel

on the first and third Mondays in each and every month. Returning, will

Leave Quesnel on Saturdays

after the first and third Mondays

For further particulars apply to

J.A. Fraser, Quesnel, or A.G. Hamilton, Fort George

A.G. Hamilton advertisement in the *Fort George Herald*, October 1909.

of what had been Central or Fort George was brought about by a terrible fire that swept through the town in November 1914. When the smoke cleared it became obvious that two hotels plus eleven stores and offices had burned to the ground.

Their biggest loss occurred, though, when they failed to get the new railway to build their facilities near Central. When the station, with its roundhouse and other assets, was built near George Street, the success of the downtown business area of Prince George was assured.

In retrospect, it seems unfair that the entire area was not called Fort George, thereby sticking with the name given it by Simon Fraser, one of the greatest explorers in the annals of this province. Perhaps it is not well known that history was not kind to the great explorer. For many years his grave at St. Andrews churchyard near Cornwall was neglected. Finally in 1921 Colonel J.T. Robinson of Kamloops, BC insisted that the grave have a monument erected by British Columbians. When Robinson visited the gravesite with ex-mayor Wells Gray of New Westminster, they found only two pieces of broken rail, and were forced to ask an elderly resident to point out the grave to them. Thoroughly upset at this discovery, the two men called on Colonel McGregor at the original homestead and learned that he had already been in touch with Sir Robert Kindersley, chairman of the Hudson's Bay Company, who had given McGregor authorization to secure a suitable monument, which was finally erected in the churchyard.

In 1909 road superintendent J. Cameron, along with a large crew of men, managed to punch through seventy-five miles of new road, such as it was, from Blackwater Crossing to South Fort George. As well, they repaired fifty miles of old road, and all for the sum of twenty thousand dollars. It was, to put it mildly, a hazardous journey along the new road. At that time there were no roadhouses of any kind throughout the sixty-mile trip to the Blackwater River.

In September 1909, pioneer merchant A.G. Hamilton started a stage line to run from Fort George to Quesnel twice a month. On his first trip south in December, it took three and a half days just to cover the sixty miles (97 km) to Blackwater Crossing, which was the point where the road crossed the Blackwater River. The temperature was

-28° C. when they left, and because there was no stopping place, they had to camp outside at night. When he finally got back to Fort George from Quesnel after another four and a half days on the return trip, he had four passengers and a supply of corsets for Kennedy's store.

The first issue of the *Fort George Tribune* carried the following story, which described Fort George at the time:

> The Fort George of today is an Indian village of 100 men, women and children, who live in log houses on an Indian Reserve of approximately 1,500 acres, with a frontage of half a mile on the Fraser and about two miles along the Nechako. Adjoining it on the south is the Hudson's Bay Company reserve of 97 acres, on which are the Company's store, manager's residence, and a few small warehouses. This land also fronts on the Fraser River. Next south is a piece of land (60 acres) owned by A.G. Hamilton [formerly of Giscome Portage] who has subdivided a portion of it into town lots. It is known as South Fort George. Here are located William Blair and Company's general store, Clarke's sawmill, and the *Tribune*'s printing office. Adjoining Hamilton's 60 acres is Joseph Thapage's pre-emption, on which Hamilton has a general store and several small buildings, and Frank Hoferkamp has a barbershop. West of the Indian Reserve are two tracts of over 100 acres each. One is called Central Fort George and lots are being sold at Vancouver for $100 each . . . The three general merchandise stores at Fort George keep very complete stocks and few articles needed by settlers are wanting.

The well-stocked stores attest to the difference the steamers made in just a short period of time. Without them, there would have been precious little in any store, and the prices would have been prohibitive.

In order to give the reader some idea of the state of isolation in the Interior at that time I want to relate a story carried in Quesnel's *Cariboo Observer* on May 22, 1909:

> W. Spittal, who left Barkerville in January on a prospecting

trip to Tête Jaune Cache accompanied by H. Henderson, Charles Baker and James McCurdy, arrived in Quesnel from Fort George last week, with both feet badly frozen. The story of the tragic deaths of Baker and McCurdy has already been told in these columns.

After leaving Barkerville they were making for a cache of supplies situated at some point on Goat River, which they finally reached, but found that it had been robbed, and was practically empty. About this time Spittal, who had frozen his feet and was unable to travel, made a camp at the mouth of Goat River, where he had been hauled on a sleigh, and where he remained while the rest of the party went in search of a party of trappers, who were supposed to be somewhere in the vicinity. Baker and McCurdy, travelling without food, had evidently become exhausted and had succumbed to the terrible hardships of the trail, as neither were properly clad and were without food. Of Henderson, nothing has yet been heard; he is supposed to have gone to Edmonton via Tête Jaune Cache. Spittal managed to reach the mouth of the Clearwater [Torpy] River alone—having amputated his toes

A.G. Hamilton's general store, later sold to Chinese merchant Ah Yee. COURTESY VIOLET BAXTER

with a butcher knife—from which point he made his way to Fort George in the company of some trappers.

Note the great number of miles covered by Spittal in his starving and injured condition. For instance, just the distance between the Clearwater River and Fort George was 164 miles (264 km) by frozen river!

It is impossible to overstate the importance of the Hudson's Bay posts prior to the arrival of the steamers and stages. Travellers, such as prospectors and trappers, often had no other place to find food and supplies in the endless wilderness of the northern Interior. Something else that drew my attention was the special status afforded the chief factors of these Hudson's Bay posts. Father Adrian Morice was a noted priest who helped the Natives a great deal throughout the Interior. He was also a famous explorer and map-maker. He wrote:

These officers, especially the Chief Factor in charge of an important post, enjoyed the greatest consideration and were treated with every mark of respect. This exalted functionary was lord paramount; his word was law; he was necessarily surrounded by a halo of dignity, and his person was sacred so to speak. He was dressed every day in a suit of black or dark blue, white shirt, collars to his ears, frock coat, velvet stock and straps to the bottom of his trousers. When he went out of doors he wore a black beaver hat worth forty shillings. When travelling in a canoe or boat, he was lifted in and out of the craft by the crew; he still wore his beaver hat, but it was protected by an oiled silk cover, and over his black frock he wore a long cloak made of Royal Stuart tartan lined with scarlet or dark blue bath coating. The cloak had a soft Genoa velvet collar, which was fastened across by mosaic gold clasps and chains. It also had voluminous capes. He carried with him an ornamental bag, technically called a "fire bag," which contained his tobacco, steel and flint, touchwood, tinderbox and brimstone matches. In camp his tent was pitched apart from the shelter given his crew. He had a separate fire, and the first duty of the boat's crew after landing was to pitch his tent, clear his camp and collect firewood sufficient for the night before they were allowed to attend to their own wants. Salutes were fired on his departure from the Fort and on his return. All this ceremony was considered necessary; it had a good effect on the Indians; it added to his dignity in the eyes of his subordinates, but sometimes spoiled the Chief Factor. Proud indeed was the Indian fortunate enough to be presented with the Chief Factor's cast-off hat, however battered it might become. He donned it on all important occasions, and in very fine weather it might constitute his entire costume.

It is not difficult to believe that some of these chief factors got spoiled with all that attention lavished upon them; however, all things considered, the ends probably justified the means.

In May 1910 a most significant event took place when the area received the first Caucasian woman, a Mrs. Fetrow. An aged homesteader who witnessed the event muttered, "Maybe now we'll get some decent cooking."

The steamer *Quesnel* at South Fort George with Mrs. Fetrow, the first Caucasian woman to arrive at Fort George. By her side—decked out in all his glory—is Hudson's Bay Factor James Cowie, May 1910. BC Archives B-00307

This man's statement should not be taken lightly; it should be no surprise that quality food was hard to find at that time.

Seven months after Mrs. Fetrow's arrival there were over fifty white women in the district. A year later the first white wedding took place in the district of Fort George.

The new opportunities presented by the arrival of the sternwheelers in the Fort George area were noted and taken advantage of by syndicates. They quickly moved into the area and grabbed large pieces of land, then tried to sell them at exorbitant profits. For example, land that cost the syndicates $3.50 to $5.00 an acre was offered at $16 an acre plus $3 cash down. Many of the incoming settlers were too smart to take the bait and instead took pre-emptions. The initial outlay for a 160-acre pre-emption was a fee of $2, with the provision that the land had to be lived on, improvements had to be made, and $1 an acre paid in four annual installments.

Even back in 1910 it became obvious that huge fortunes had been squandered away by people who didn't pursue their land claims. This was plainly pointed out by an article in the *Fort George Herald* dated September 17, 1910:

> Strange to say, several prior stakings had been made on the land, but none of the applicants had gone any further than to drive a location post on the ground that is now decorated by thousands of corner posts of twenty-five-foot lots. Amongst these prior locators was Bob Alexander, one of the oldest residents of this place, who staked land, but through inattention to the necessary procedure, awoke one morning to find that his time for application had lapsed. Both men were in the employ of the Grand Trunk Pacific [Railway], who never went any further than to stake.
>
> The Victoria owner did not hold the land long, selling it for $75 an acre. The buyer, a Winnipeg operator named Campbell, sold it to Hugo Ross and an associate for $175 an acre.
>
> The present value of the land is estimated at $250,000.00, which value is of course based on the sale prices of the lots held in joint ownership by the Natural Resources Company and Hugo Ross.

An investment by some of those old stakers in a two-cent stamp would have netted a very fair margin of profit, but that is the history of the entire Fort George vicinity in retrospect for the past two or three years. The woods around here are full of these "if I had of—" gentlemen, but we shed never a tear.

At a time when wages were less than two dollars a day, the sums of money involved were breathtaking to say the least.

During the summer of 1910, pioneer explorer and cook Ernie Pinker constructed a much-needed roadhouse between Fort George and Blackwater Crossing. Built at 38-Mile, it was capable of housing eighteen people and had a barn that held eighteen horses. This prepared the area for the arrival of the big stages of the BC Express Company.

It was also in 1910 that the steamer *B.X.* came upriver with 138,000 pounds of freight. At the same time the steamer *Chilco* arrived with a load of freight for Seebach and Huble at Giscome Portage, forty-one miles (66 km) upriver from Fort George. For some reason the steamers were not allowed to carry gasoline, possibly because of the fire hazard. This created many problems for people using gasoline

First Street, South Fort George 1910. Note that some of the buildings are built from scow timbers. COURTESY VIOLET BAXTER

33

engines for any purpose. The situation was alleviated somewhat by the freighters who moved gasoline in overland on sleighs or wagons.

Another memorable first for the area was noted in the *Fort George Tribune* on August 6, 1910:

> Fort George is now on the map in regard to modern means of communication. In the face of difficulties and setbacks, chiefly owing to the inability to get the necessary material on the ground, the telephone line of the Fort George-Alberta Telephone Co. reached Fort George today. Though not yet connected with the company's office here [South Fort George] the line is already doing a good business. By Monday, or Tuesday at the latest, the main office of the company on Central Avenue, Fort George, will be open for business, and the branch line over to South Fort George will be commenced . . . All that will be necessary now for the people of Fort George to communicate with outside points will be to call up the telegraph operator at Blackwater Crossing and dictate the message to him. It will then be immediately transmitted over the Dominion Government telegraph line to its destination.

During 1910, the abundance of people heading to the Georges put an unbearable strain on everything, as testified to by the *Herald* on August 6, 1910:

> Almost the moment spring opened up, hundreds [of people] rushed into the country. The existing transportation facilities broke down utterly under the pressure. Hundreds got no further than Ashcroft; hundreds more did not get past Quesnel. None of these people got within a hundred miles of the place they had come, in many cases great distances, to see. And those who did endure the hardships and delays necessary to a disorganized and inefficient system of travel found on their arrival that the town could neither properly feed nor sleep them. Under those conditions it required much both of faith and fortitude to continue to strongly believe in the future destiny of a city that gave its well-wishers such discomforts

in travelling to view it, and such a chilling reception on their arrival.

The enormous pressure put on the fledgling community was handled much better than expected. In a short period of time hotels and rooming houses flourished and made the travellers welcome, though some of the so-called "stopping places" were just that. There were bedrooms just large enough to contain a bed. Often the room had no door, just a curtain. One traveller expressed disbelief when he crawled into a bed that was still warm from the previous occupant.

Another example of the freighting problems faced by the pioneers occurred in October 1910 when Ed Seebach of Giscome Portage came downriver with one of Green and Burden's survey parties. He was chasing about a ton of expected supplies that had gone missing somewhere along the road between Soda Creek and his store.

Sometimes the poor communication between Fort George and the outside world led to confusion. Such was the case for Johnson and Burns, owners of the newly built Northern Hotel in South Fort George with its famous seventy-foot bar. The Alberta Telephone Company had just succeeded in getting phone service to the area when a windstorm blew some of the poles over. As soon as the service was restored an order went out for some liquor. In its December 17, 1910, edition the *Herald* noted:

> South Fort George is without the proverbial liquor of the Honourable Adventurers—Scotch—just because the Alberta Telephone Company's office happens to be located in the woods, away from the busy hum of business. A message was sent to Quesnel, to a wholesale and retail dealer, at the time of the granting of the [liquor] licence to Johnson and Burns of the Northern Hotel, which read, "Load Cannon up with Scotch and beer and forward."
>
> Frank Cannon, the freighter, had written instructions for the shipment, and when he called on the wholesaler, the latter produced a telegram which read, "Load canoe up with Scotch and beer and forward."
>
> The shipment was not delivered to Cannon, but in its

stead, placed in a canoe, and today is on the long Fraser, some-where between the brewing centre and South Fort George. Result? Dry weather with an absence of Scotch.

It was merely an accident in transmission, and something that is likely to occur in the best regulated telephone office.

It reminds the writer of another "slip of the ear" which occurred last month, when a message from J. Charleson, dated Chicago, U.S.A., asking for the first publication of a certain land notice, turned out to be "Nechako" instead of "Chicago."

Another story was told to me by Prince George historian Ted Williams, who heard it from his father. A canoe-load of booze was lost along the river for about ten days. When it arrived in South Fort George it was short a substantial amount of liquor. The canoeists claimed that they had an accident that resulted in the loss of the missing booze, but a southbound canoeist named John Fountain had a different tale. He said that after he passed the Cottonwood Canyon he heard sounds of revelry emanating from the forest, where a long canoe was tied up. The two stories likely refer to the same event, and it appears obvious that for a period of at least a week it was party time on the Fraser River. Surprisingly, to me at least, the December newspaper date shows that the Fraser River was still open to travel at that time of year. This seems to indicate that there were mild winters back then.

In his book *The New Garden of Canada*, Fred Talbot describes Fort George in August 1910:

Ample recreation was provided in the poolroom, where snooker, Boston and pyramids held sway. When the frequent-ers grew tired of cue and ivories the tables were pushed into a corner and vent was found for exuberance in dancing to the strains of a wheezy, expiring gramophone, in footwear, which could scarcely be described as ballroom, for heavy hobnailed half-inch soles clattered over the uneven knotty boards. Opposite was a small gambling hall presided over by a Chinaman, whence continually issued, "Hit me! Hit me again!" as blackjack was briskly played, with poker and other games of chance. This saloon was a certain outlet for money, and as Johnny is an inveterate gambler, participating with a keen gusto in the games, always winning, he was acquiring a pretty long and weighted stocking. To play a game of

Pioneer John McInnis arrived at South Fort George in 1910 on the steamer *Chilco*. COURTESY GEORGINA WILLIAMS

chance with a Chinaman is like pitting oneself against an automatic machine. There was one worthy who was possessed of some fine horses, one of which was always hitched to the doorpost. It stood there for hours while its owner was inside trying to win fortune with the cards. Presently there would be a hubbub. The player emerged having lost everything. "Here! How much for the plug?" drawing attention to his horse. "Give me $80! What, too much! Well, say $70! No good! $60! Fifty! Gee-whiz, you are a lot of robbers! Who says $40?"

Eventually the horse would trade hands for about $30, and armed with the greenbacks, the gambler once more disappeared exultantly into the saloon. When he won—and he did often and heavily at that—he came out, and bought back his horse for double the price he had received. If he lost he simply staggered back to his tent, to reappear the next day with another animal and repeat the same round. While officially "dry," the town was actually "wetter" than a licensed community bristling with gin palaces. Drink was freely smuggled in, while "rock cut" was brewed extensively in a certain quarter and vended as "Hudson's Bay Rum" to secure a steady sale, this being the most famous drink in the west. It was as

The Hotel Northern, scene of many brutal fights. COURTESY VIOLET BAXTER

much like Hudson's Bay Rum as salad oil is like Chartreuse. The opium or nicotine juice with which it was saturated provoked intoxication in the shortest possible space of time, and the Indians were to be seen on every hand staggering and reeling under its baleful influence. The larger well-ordered section of the community endeavoured to check this abuse, but to no avail.

Mr. Talbot's assessment of the situation was backed up by many of the town's leading people. In a letter to Quesnel's *Cariboo Observer* Francis Hoferkamp, a barber from South Fort George, wrote:

Following are a few facts concerning Fort George. For the past two years, illicit liquor has been sold by the glass, bottle or just as you like it. A person can get one or two cases at any time, as long as you have the cash in your pocket, or you can even get it charged up for you, for it comes upriver in wholesale quantities, consequently there has been no danger of a drought here. This illicit selling is an everyday occurrence. At night the howls of the red man intermingle with those of the whites, and occasionally to break the monotony, you can hear the reports of a pistol or shotgun, and it's all in dead earnest. The trail between lower and upper Fort George, in the wintertime, is trampled down 20 feet wide and there you can see the resting places of many poor victims of excess . . .

The goings-on complained about by Mr. Hoferkamp were just a warm-up for what was to occur with the arrival of the Grand Trunk Pacific Railway construction crews that were to descend on Fort George a few years later. When these "gandy dancers" arrived, the town really got rough.

One of my biggest surprises while gathering material for this book was the great number of surveyors working in the forests in 1910. Many were plotting out possible railway lines as well as surveying the land for the new settlers who were arriving in droves. What may not be known, though, is that there were many other survey projects going as well, such as the proposed Willow River and Barkerville Railroad that was surveyed but never came to fruition.

The crowning achievement of the year 1910 was the birth of the first Caucasian baby in the area, born November 17 in South Fort George. She was the daughter of John and Fanny McInnis and was named Fort Georgina after the town of South Fort George. Annie Huble of Giscome Portage fame was the midwife attendant at her birth.

I spent an interesting afternoon chatting with Georgina, who still resides in Prince George at the time of this writing. Georgina's memories go back a long way, to her childhood in Prince George. It is a delight to listen as she relives the past. Her father, the well-known businessman John McInnis, who arrived in 1910 on the sternwheeler *Chilco*, was one of Prince George's great pioneers.

I questioned Georgina about her name and she admitted that it was a burden at times, such as the first day she entered the Royal Conservatory of Music in Toronto, where she eventually earned a degree. Just past the entrance, she found a list of all the attendees, and among them was listed her name, "Fort McInnis." It didn't take very long for her to get the "Fort" part of her name discarded permanently.

Georgina put her knowledge of music to good use, teaching thousands of students over a period of seventy years.

"When I was fourteen," Georgina recalls, "I played music in the theatres on George Street during the silent movies. The people who ran the theatres sent me sheets of music and told me what to play during the shows, but it didn't always work out. I remember the time I was playing jazz when a dog appeared to be howling on the screen. People enjoyed it, though, because there was so little entertainment in those days."

Some of the newspaper editorials of those times were priceless beyond words. The wry humour is startling. One such article was taken from the October 1, 1910, edition of the *Herald*. It described the deceased editor of the rival newspaper, the *Fort George Tribune*, which was located in South Fort George:

The little cabin in which the *Tribune* first saw the light of day has disappeared and gone the way of all primitive northern bungalows. Mr. Walker purchased the building from the original owner of the town-site, A.G. Hamilton, and on Monday razed it to the ground. The dimensions of the little canvas-covered cabin were 10 x 12 [feet], and in it John Houston had the most compact little printing plant that ever graced the confines of isolated sections. It was a departmental store in the woods. It comprised a restaurant, a rooming house, a drug store, a carpenter shop, a library, a bindery, and the publishing office of an unprivileged-mail weekly newspaper. The editor was the head of all these departments. He composed as he stood at the solitary frame. He decomposed in a sitting posture. He washed his forms with water taken from the Fraser; lit his perpetual fire in a small box stove; swept out all the departments every morning; packed his coal-oil from Kennedy's store; filled his one little oil lamp, and polished its chimney three times a day. At meal hours he spread a sheet of paper over the imposing stone and stood up at his meals—bacon and beans, coffee and cakes. There was not one minute lost in the long day that went into the early hours of the morning. He worked out 1909, and worked in 1910, by setting new 6-point by lamplight. He did the same on Christmas Eve. He attended to correspondence numbering 300 letters per month. He was scrupulously particular about his mailing list and his books. With all this he found time to formulate a platform for the Progressive Liberal Party of British Columbia, and all this from a man of sixty-one years. Is it any wonder that he succumbed? And now this abode of Houston has been dismembered for the sake of disposing of the dozen planks the structure contained for commercial purposes. Had the big-hearted owner of this priceless landmark but revolved the thought in his inner self, he would have left to posterity an emblem that would have stimulated the unborn thousands and spurred them on to emulate the actions of one who knew not the meaning of the word failure.

With men such as this leading and inspiring others, how could the new town possibly fail?

Another memorable event was described by John B. "Jack" Daniell, owner of the *Fort George Herald*. Along with two pioneer merchants, Close and Brown, Jack had built a theatre adjacent to the great Northern Hotel in order to capitalize on the hotel trade. In 1910 the hotel was destroyed in a fire. The new hotel was then erected at the opposite end of town, so the three entrepreneurs were forced to cut the theatre in half, move it across town and set it up near the new hotel site. Even back then, "location" was an all-important word.

A trip to Fort George usually started at Ashcroft, on the Canadian Pacific Railway. From there it was a stagecoach ride to Soda Creek, and then a ride by steamer to Fort George. This occupied two and a

Fort George Theatre about 1911. COURTESY VIOLET BAXTER

half days by stage and then two days' travel upriver by steamer. For a time the British Columbia General Transportation Company attempted to put steam-driven three-wheeled coaches on the two runs between Yale and Soda Creek and Yale and Barkerville. The venture was a failure, though, because the vehicles were unable to pull coaches up steep hills.

F. J. Barnard operated stagecoaches from Ashcroft to Fort George and also owned the sternwheelers *B.X.* and *BC Express*. At one time, Barnard's old company the BC Express (known popularly as the B.X.), had two hundred horses on the stage line. About 1911 they started switching to automobiles, which provided a much faster and more comfortable delivery system.

Something that tickled my sense of humour was the means of transportation used around the Georges, such as the one mentioned in the *Fort George Tribune* of January 7, 1911:

> Dog teams are the popular motive power at present for those making trips to distant parts of the district. Every ki-yi that can make a noise like a dog is hustled into service. Wun Lung, the Chinese laundryman, has a team composed of a collie and an Irish terrier which he uses to transport washes to his patrons.

Another article concerning dogs appeared in November 1911 in the *Herald*:

> Life in Fort George is nothing if not interesting and there's always something doing to prevent the appetite for excitement from becoming jaded. Now it's dogs. For the past week or so the dogs from the adjoining Indian Reservation have deserted their usual haunts for the chances of forage to be had in this town and daylight and dark have been filled with the music of these concert performers.
>
> It has not all been music either and more than one stock of provisions has suddenly disappeared to show up in the well filled expressions worn on the faces of a dozen or so half-bred huskies . . .

The writer went on to point out that now that snow covered the ground, the Natives were out looking for their dogs, which they needed to pull their sleds. He added that they were having difficulty retrieving the dogs because they had grown used to a good thing.

Another event that often amused the populace concerned a man called "Red" Killoran. Red drove a horse-drawn taxi that made regular trips between the two Georges, Fort and South Fort, a three-mile run. It was well known to townsfolk that Red had a weakness, in that he frequently imbibed to the point where he would fall asleep at the controls. This didn't seem to interfere with business because the horse knew the route so well that it would continue on until Red regained consciousness, often to find that the honest travellers had slipped the fare money into his pockets as he slept.

A B.X. Company advertisement from the *Fort George Herald* for autos, stages and steamboats.

Without question the most anticipated event of the year in the Georges was the arrival of the first steamer of the season, which was well depicted in the following excerpt taken from the *Herald* of May 13, 1911:

The first boat of the season has arrived and departed. The welcome roar of her whistle awakened the echoes on Monday evening when Captain Browne of the big steamer *B.X.* opened the blast throttle opposite Fort George Centre. It brought the populace scrambling from their beds to welcome the opening event in linking up the metropolis of the North with the outside world. For six months past, communication between this point and the outer world has been solely by way of a sleigh road 320 miles (515 km) in length. This condition of winter travel will remain in force until the completion of the Grand Trunk Pacific Railroad in two years time. The last boat left here on November 6th last year. That boat was the ill-fated steamer *Chilco*, wrecked in Cottonwood Canyon two weeks ago whilst being taken to Quesnel for repairs.

Amidst scenes of the wildest excitement the *B.X.* came to her landing on Monday evening. The population—men, women and children—were en-masse on the landing in spite

The steamer *B.X.* at the Hudson's Bay fort, Fort George, BC, 1910. BC Archives A-08056

of the lateness of the hour. As the big boat drew into her slip, wild cheering mingled with the sounds of the bell signals issuing from her engine room, and the pant of the compound engine's exhausts. The passenger deck and bow space were crowded with over a hundred passengers. J.W. West, manager of the BC Express Company, owners of the boat, stated that the boat had brought up all the passengers bound for Fort George from Soda Creek and Quesnel. There were many people on the way, said Mr. West, though efforts had been made to hold back the rush until the boats were in commission. All the accommodation on the B.X. is booked for several trips ahead, according to information from an official of the Company. In addition to the heavy passenger list the boat landed 85,000 pounds of freight, consigned principally to South Fort George. The B.X. is in splendid shape for a heavy season's work. She has been thoroughly overhauled, previous to launching, and is manned by capable personnel of officers and men. Captain Browne, her commander, is the pioneer captain of the upper Fraser run. All the officers this year are adorned in brand-new bound uniforms with red facings—some class.

The *Herald* wishes the B.X. a most successful season. Last week we expressed some doubt as to whether the mail would come through as wires received from Quesnel stated that the boat was still on the ways [a base for launching huge boats]; possibly the sender had a skate on and mistook the old *Charlotte* for the B.X. We take it all back—something we have never done before—the old reliable has delivered the goods as heretofore, and we stand humbled and abashed before the multitude.

Many of the passengers that arrived on the B.X. had a strange tale to tell about their journey over the Cariboo Trail. When informed by the BC Express Company that their luggage was limited to forty pounds per person, they became creative and placed their extra possessions in gunny sacks. For some strange reason the goods were accepted and delivered without question.

Another first for South Fort George was featured in the *Herald* of October 21, 1911:

For the first time in history the stages of the British Columbia Stage Company rolled into South Fort George on Thursday last. The big red coaches drawn by four splendid horses showed signs of the hard trip they had made over the rough and uncompleted road between here and Quesnel. Drivers Fred Peters and Al Young do not complain of that portion of the road that lies between South Fort George and Blackwater, but they state that for the big coaches the road between Blackwater and Quesnel is altogether impracticable and dangerous. Both the drivers are experts at handling the ribbons [reins] and are old-timers on the Cariboo Road service. The stages brought in 25 bags of mail and seven passengers. The service will not be so difficult to run with the smaller sleighs the company will use on their winter service. But the wheel rigs, which they have impressed into the service during the interrupted navigation [low water stopped the steamers] will have great difficulty in making the trip on any kind of schedule. The stages made good time on the

Six-horse team and stagecoach at South Fort George, 1912. E. Sinclair photo

road, leaving Quesnel on Monday morning and landing here
Thursday at 4 p.m.

The arrival of the stagecoach was a huge step forward for the area.
Though it may seem impossible that the stage line ran during the
deep snows of mid-winter, nonetheless it certainly did.

The stagecoach trip was by no means a pleasure jaunt, as attested
to by a man known as Mr. Senior, who received a dislocation of his
lower jaw when the driver portaged over a log in the trail. The next
year a woman was similarly injured. It is not difficult to understand
why the residents anxiously awaited the railroad.

Whenever we feel that we are having a bad day, perhaps because
we are stuck in a traffic jam for an hour, we should look back at what
the pioneers had to put up with, such as when low water levels in the
river stopped the steamers from travelling. This meant that sometimes
the residents went months without getting mail or supplies. After the
stages arrived in South Fort George, everyone expected better, and let
it be known. An editorial viewpoint was carried in the *Herald* dated
October 21, 1911:

> When a town is situated geographically 300 miles from the
> nearest railroad point, which is a condition affecting this
> place today, every convenience that can be afforded it by the
> governments should be forthcoming freely and dependably,
> as a reasonable measure of assistance to the pioneers who are
> developing by their energy and ambition, the hinterlands of
> the country which those governments are administering. For
> two solid weeks the people here did not receive their mail
> until the mail contractors sent in the congested accumulation
> over the wagon road by their stages. The mail contractors
> have no legal right to delay the people's mail . . .

In a long-winded diatribe, the editor got the point across that
people were not satisfied with the low-water excuse. It seemed reasonable to expect that regardless of how many stagecoaches were required, that many should be available to get the mail through in a
reasonable amount of time.

The large number of people pre-empting north of the Nechako River by November 1912 was demonstrated when the ferry across the Nechako closed for the season after a hectic summer's schedule. It had been so busy that at times it became swamped as it moved pre-emptors and ranchers across the river. Many were just speculators checking the suitability of land well north of the Nechako River. In fact, the area about thirty miles (48 km) north of Prince George was referred to as Starvation Flats because many of the early-day farmers gave up and relocated. In fairness to this area, I must point out that it was renowned for its huckleberries, and still is.

The other reaction ferry—a ferry that is attached to a cable and propelled across the river by the force of the water against the rudders—installed in 1910, crossed the Fraser River near the Hudson's Bay slough. It was also busy moving people back and forth across the river. Pre-emptors were taking up the available land wherever it was capable of growing a crop. Luther Collins Gunn, famed surveyor of the GTP Railway, chose the homestead just east of the river on what is now the Moffat Ranch. "L.C." as he was called, was one of the most famous surveyors in the history of this province. His exploits are legend and it is doubtful that many surveyors covered more ground in British Columbia than he did.

The toughness of these pioneers was often exhibited in the trips they took to and from this area. Just an example of what misery the stage drivers and their clientele had to put up with is described in this article in the *Fort George Weekly Herald* on November 16, 1912:

> The first big load of freight brought in over the road from Quesnel since the steamers stopped their service on the Fraser, arrived on Tuesday afternoon when W.R. Bookhout pulled in with a four-horse team and 5,200 pounds of hardware stock behind it. This is Mr. Bookhout's first trip of the season, and as he has something like 44,000 pounds in the Quesnel and Soda Creek warehouses. There will be some hauling done over the route between here and the two lower river points before the shelves of his store are filled with the orders he has on the way.
>
> Speaking of the roads between here and Quesnel, Mr.

Bookhout says they are about as bad now as they possibly could be. Before the recent frosts, the rains of the fall had softened the beds till the wagons cut in at some places a foot and a half deep. Now the frosts have put in their stroke and the ruts are as hard as rock, the result being a wagon route in spots that takes in every bit of the wheels up to the hubs. The outfit that arrived Thursday started with more than 7,000 pounds aboard, but about 2,000 of this proved a bit too strong for the going the other side of Blackwater, so it was cached along the way for the next trip . . . On Wednesday evening three other loads arrived when a trio of Corbett's teams pulled in from down the road with mixed consignments of merchandise for Fort George. In these lots were several thousand pounds for Peters & Stretch, gentlemen's furnishers; new machinery for Pooley Bros.' Sash & Door factory, including a sander, planer, etc.; some for the *Tribune* and several smaller lots for different consignees about town. All the drivers report the heaviest kind of hauling along the way with bad roads in most places and worse in the remainder.

Many of the new arrivals to the Georges had purchased land on speculation, such as the man who arrived to find that he had bought a piece of the sandhill across the Nechako River. When a passerby inquired as to why he looked so glum, he replied, "I spent all my money on that piece of land over there and every time one of those slides come down I lose about fifty dollars. I figure I've lost about two hundred dollars since nine o'clock this morning. I don't know whether to jump in the river or go back east and sell the lots to my brother-in-law before they are all washed away."

This gentleman was just one of many who were taken in by crooked promoters.

There were a few that should have been called dreamers rather than promoters, such as the man who purchased some land in the middle of nowhere northeast of the Georges in a place he named Fraser City. In an attempt to sell his lots, this individual claimed that nine different railroads were going to intersect his property. His so-called city was located four miles north of Willow River and across the Fraser River from the GTP Railway. Understandably this city never amounted to anything.

At this same time, 1912, another group of promoters from Vancouver purchased and subdivided some land that they called Willow City. The GTP purchased another block and called it Willow River. Caught in the middle, George Hartford, editor of the *Willow River Times*, tried to walk a fine balancing act between the rival towns, which both claimed to represent the area. An end was put to that nonsense when the post office got fed up with all the different names and declared that the post office address would be Willow River.

These Willow City promoters went whole hog and claimed that three railways were going to intersect their property while eight others would approach the area. It must have taken incredible willpower to turn down such rosy offers as this.

The exaggeration used by these promoters is made plain by these examples, but the Georges went one better when a Fort George promoter claimed that eleven railroads were to converge on his property. The warning "buyer beware" was never more applicable than during the years 1910 to 1915 in the area of the Georges.

This news item is taken from the *Vancouver Province* dated November 26, 1910:

> A survey for a proposed electric railway between Barkerville and Fort George was completed last week. The route is via the

The steamers *Chilcotin, BC Express* and *B.X.* at South Fort George, 1913.
COURTESY GUS LUND

valley of the Willow River, a distance of about 150 miles (242 km). The party was in charge of Mr. Murphy of Vancouver. It is said construction operations will be started next spring. A water power will be developed to supply the electrical energy for operating the line."

No mention was made of the enormous outlay of capital required to fund such a venture, possibly because there was no intent to pursue it.

On another occasion a mother with two daughters arrived in the Georges. An unscrupulous Vancouver real-estate dealer had told them that there were two thousand people in Fort George, so they ventured north with the intent of opening a boarding house. Heartbroken when they learned the truth, the three women were on the next steamer heading south.

The people of Fort George got a surprise in July 1910 when a woman named Irene Jordan let it be known that she was going to open a house of ill repute. The *Tribune* editor summed up his feelings thus, " . . . If the people of Fort George want brothels—let them have brothels—this is the *Tribune's* opinion."

The editor went on to point out that the police would not be able to prevent a scattering of houses if they allowed one. Police Chief Daunt, for his part, seemed to be in favour of the brothel so long as it was segregated from the general community.

Emboldened by the apparent agreement, Irene Jordan bought six lots at the corner of Seventh Avenue and Cariboo Street. Next she had an elaborate building erected and furnished. Scarcely five weeks from the date of purchase Miss Jordan opened for business.

In the interim, Chief Daunt had received a promotion and moved. In his place came W.R. Dunwoody, whose first order of business was to close down the "disorderly house" that had opened on the night of his arrival. The *Tribune's* headline read: "House Opened in Fort George Closed on Evening of Opening."

We can but wonder how many disillusioned young men had their wildest dreams destroyed that evening. We must also wonder why Miss Jordan didn't get something in writing before investing so much money in this endeavour. The answer to this question was carried in the rival newspaper, the *Fort George Herald*, when it charged "influential interests" in Fort George with promising protection for the ladies of the night. Far from discouraged, Miss Jordan and several others of her trade simply moved to a segregated area and opened for business.

Another incident of note took place in June 1913 when Reverend C.M. Wright of Fort George addressed a Toronto gathering of Presbyterians. The next day a Toronto newspaper carried the headline: "Walked 350 Miles From the Very Gates of Hell."

When asked what particular form of vice was rampant in Fort George, the minister replied, "In the first place the liquor traffic is flourishing. There are two saloons with four to six bartenders each. The bankers have told me their deposits have dwindled with the granting of licences. Then there is the segregated district, four big houses with thirty women, in South Fort George, two blocks from Knox Church. The police formerly had no authority to raid the houses, now one has been fined."

The minister rather sheepishly defended a watered-down version of the story, but the two area newspapers, the *Fort George Herald* and the *Fort George Tribune*, were incensed to put it mildly. One editor wrote:

> Once, in Vancouver, it is alleged that the Rev. Mr. Wright preached a sermon in which he left his congregation impressed with the idea that Fort George was a regular Circe of cities; a place where lust and vice walked untrammelled; where the people mocked religion and abetted wickedness and evil deeds. Mr. Wright strives to obliterate sin from the surface. He would drive out houses of prostitution; he would close up hotel bars and would make religion compulsory. This sort of thing has all been tried before. It gives way to illicit liquor traffic; to the erection of foundling hospitals for misbegotten children, and to atheism.

More than just a bit humbled, Mr. Wright admitted that his so-called "350-mile trek" had actually been made by steamer and automobile.

During the summers of 1912 and 1913, a great many railroad

workers descended on the Georges. Often the steamers were loaded with hundreds of construction workers looking for excitement on their days off.

The new Northern Hotel with its ninety-foot bar (the first one with its famous seventy-foot bar burned down in 1910) and twenty-four bartenders was at times a scene of utter bedlam. Drinks cost twenty-five cents and the buyer had a choice of either one or two drinks for that price. One day in 1911 the bar sold seven thousand drinks. Often the patrons were five deep at the bar. This meant that the men at the back of the pile had to have their money pass through several hands to get to the till. As well, the drinks had to pass through several hands to get back to the purchasers. Many times the money didn't get to the bartenders, or "mixologists" as they were jokingly referred to, before someone pocketed it. The drinks, of course, had even less chance of getting back to the purchasers before they were partially or completely consumed. This led to many altercations, some of which lasted for hours until the police rushed to the hotel to break things up. Just how out of control the situation got at times was made plain on a night in January 1913 when nineteen people were taken to jail for being drunk and disorderly.

The following story from the *Herald* of May 31, 1913 illustrates what the police faced:

> A man named Kilpatrick, a giant in stature and strength, precipitated a small riot in the Northern Hotel last Thursday night by refusing to leave the bar room when ordered to by the house policeman Charlie Wylie. Wylie, who is also a big man, closed with the scow-man and a battle of giants opened fast and furious. Kilpatrick was thrown out about the time police appeared on the scene. He resisted arrest and a free-for-all fight started. Chief Daunt and his men had great difficulty in preventing a serious riot among the foreigners who closed in on them, and they were forced to draw their guns, but handled the difficult situation with credit. Kilpatrick was taken to the lockup. He was fined $50 or three months in jail, on a charge of creating a disturbance.

Charlie Wylie was more than just a noted bouncer; most certainly he was a truly courageous person. The following year he was assisting a police officer in the arrest of a crazy gambler when his luck ran out. Charlie banged on the door of the gambler's hotel room and ordered him to come out. Instead, the gambler fired his gun through the closed door. Mortally wounded, Charlie broke down the door and shot the man dead before succumbing to his own wounds.

Four months later in another foolish act, a man named Henry Hackman was attacked while running his fruit and tobacco stand on the river in front of the Hudson's Bay post. For no apparent reason, a drunken Pole named Aaron Vedek attacked Henry with an axe and almost severed one of his arms. Only the intervention of bystanders prevented a fatality. When the police arrived and attempted an arrest, they were assaulted by Vedek, along with his brother and a friend. The end result of that fracas was some jail time for all three men. The injured Hackman was taken to hospital with fractures of both bones in his lower arm as well as much damage to the muscles and ligaments.

It wasn't all doom and gloom, though, as there were always events taking place to lift people's spirits. In July 1913 the *Herald* noted:

> The successful navigation of the Giscome Rapids and the Grand Canyon this week by the large steamboats [*Operator* and *Conveyor*] marks an epoch in the new transportation regime. For the first time in history a cargo of merchandise came alongside of the South Fort George dock this week bearing the marks of Edmonton shippers . . .

These two big boats, the *Operator* under Captain Myers, and the *Conveyor* under Captain Shannon, frequently did the impossible, such as climbing the Nechako River for a distance of seventy miles. When they passed through a narrow spot in one of the canyons there was only about ten feet of clearance on each side of the boats, leaving precious little margin for error.

During the winter of 1912–1913 supplies ran short in the Georges because low water levels forced an early end to river navigation. In an effort to assure people that this would not happen again, the following notice was carried in the *Herald* of August 16, 1913:

Last fall a rumour was spread that food supplies were short in South Fort George and that great hunger and destitution would prevail before spring, which was to a certain extent true on account of our extreme isolation, and the early closing of navigation. This caused many of our citizens to leave for the winter, and caused complete stagnation in the influx of settlers arriving here. We would like to state here that the Kennedy-Blair Company have taken due precaution against similar conditions this year. Since the opening of navigation we have imported one thousand tons of merchandise. The transit of this vast tonnage is in the hands of our famous scow-men, Admiral George Williams, R. [Bob] Alexander and W. McLaren. We therefore issue a cordial invitation to our citizens to remain here. We also extend this invitation to people from all parts of the world who anticipate a trip to Fort George, either for business purposes or investment, to come and bring along your friends.

This notice must have lifted the spirits of all the people so dependent on supplies.

Something I found interesting was that once emptied, these scows were torn apart and used in house construction. As well, the crates that the supplies were shipped in were used for insulation in the new houses. Newspapers, too, were used for insulation. One gentleman who demolished one of these original homes stated that he found an abundance of newspapers dated 1910 through 1912.

Something else that frequently lifted spirits was "cruising" the three miles of road between South Fort George and Central or Fort George as it was called. It must have been quite a feeling of elation for the first individuals to own sporty new cars. In an effort to show off his new Ford touring car, Mr. C.B. Wark pulled out of South Fort George on December 9, 1913, bound for Vancouver. By three in the afternoon they telephoned that they were at Blackwater and expected to make Quesnel by ten that night. When the travel time was compared to the never-ending trip with horses, it was no wonder that car sales took off in the Georges.

After the enormous amount of work that had been available during railway construction, there was a downturn that followed. This led to hard times for many men. The editor of the *Prince George Post* took up this subject in the February 6, 1915 edition:

> Some cases of distress which deserve relief have been brought to the notice of the *Post*, and, although distress is not so acute here as in most places, that should be all the more reason why those cases which do exist should receive prompt and effective attention.
>
> This does not seem to have been done with a case in Central Fort George. A man who had once been foreman of construction work on the GTP Railway was in hard circumstances and was told to make application for help to a church organization. For some reason, however, no help was forthcoming from that quarter. He then turned his attention hopefully to Prince George and was sent to the relief committee. Here, again, he was refused assistance—not because the committee had no funds on hand, but because the man did not live in a cabin. He was told that because he did not have his abode in that particular kind of building, food could not be supplied him.
>
> If living in a cabin makes a difference and counts for

Steamer *Conveyor* with a load of revellers. BC Archives G-03259

more in a case of this kind than real, genuine, deserving want, The *Post* publishes this so that those who may wish to make application for aid in future will not make the fatal mistake of living in a common house, tent, or any kind of building except a cabin.

Perhaps it is fitting to end this chapter with a story from the great Reverend Adrian Gabriel Morice, who spent so many years among the Native people. Since most people in his flock were Natives, he developed his own method for dealing with them. One of his favourite memories concerned the time a young brave wanted to go to Prince George to get married but was afraid the river would freeze over before he returned. The good father looked up the weather records and realized that there should be ten more days before the river froze over. "Give me ten dollars, Peter," he said, "and be sure to be back in ten days."

Three days after Peter and his bride started on their return journey the river froze over and they were forced to cache their canoe and continue on foot. Several days later they arrived at the settlement somewhat exhausted and Peter challenged the priest, "I gave you ten dollars, Father, and you did not keep the river open for me."

Father Morice countered with, "But I told you, Peter, to remain in Prince George only ten days, and you stayed fourteen. I could not wait longer than twelve days because there were a hundred trappers here awaiting departure; I could not hold up their business any longer for the sake of one man."

The Grand Canyon

The best place to start the story of the enormous sacrifices made along the upper Fraser River is in the Grand Canyon. About two kilometres in length, this canyon 103 miles (166 km) up the Fraser River from Fort George (later named Prince George) had several surprises in store for first-time visitors.

Just around the first curve in the upper rapids was Green's Rock, which was the single largest cause of death to early river travellers. The origin of its name appears uncertain, but one old-timer said it was so named because a surveyor named Green drowned there about 1908. From the time that scow or raft operators first spotted this large rock, it was only a matter of seconds until impact. During periods of high water the current was so fast that they had little warning time.

As well, there were two small sets of falls surrounded by large boulders in the upper canyon that took their toll of rafts, scows and canoes during periods of low water; these boulders were blown away by Frank Freeman in 1912.

Once through to the lake between the upper and lower rapids, many travellers thought that the danger was past, but just around the bend in the lower rapids sat a whirlpool that stretched clear across the river during periods of high water. Many small vessels were pulled down into its seething vortex; often nothing resurfaced.

The first people to learn the power of this canyon were the Natives, who travelled the river in canoes for countless generations. Possibly the first record of travellers through the canyon occurred in 1820 when an officer for the Hudson's Bay Company named Colin Robertson sent a party of Iroquois trappers from Fort McLeod on McLeod Lake through to Tête Jaune Cache.

The first documented activity along the upper river by a non-Native appears to have been in 1825, when the Hudson's Bay Company employed a man named James McMillan to survey a trail from Jasper House, Alberta, to the head of the Fraser River. This route was used to bring leather from the Saskatchewan District as far as Tête Jaune Cache, where a rendezvous was made with two canoes sent from New Caledonia headquarters at Fort St. James, BC. Since big-game animals were scarce in north central BC at that time, this leather was in great demand. This trade route was abandoned in 1831 for a less treacherous route to the north.

Surveyors taking a loaded scow up through the Grand Canyon, passing Green's Rock, c. 1909. Courtesy Olive Williams

While it is probably a safe bet that some of these traders were lost in the swirling waters of the Grand Canyon, I have not been able to find evidence of any.

On March 18, 1827, a man named George McDougall left Fort St. James and travelled up the Fraser River to Tête Jaune Cache, a distance of over four hundred miles (640 km). After an incredibly tough trip travelling on ice and through deep snow, he reached Jasper House, Alberta on April 18 in a near-death state.

In Reverend A.G. Morice's book *The History of the Northern Interior of British Columbia*, he states that twenty-six servants of the Hudson's Bay Company came from Norway House, Alberta through Tête Jaune to the Fraser River where they met a party of New Caledonians from Fort George. The year was 1836. New Caledonia was an area that stretched from about 51°30' to 57° north latitude between the Coast and Rocky Mountains.

The fact that other individuals made their way along the upper river is also apparent because on occasion they left evidence, such as the four prospectors that left the Cariboo in 1860 and followed the Fraser River past Fort George. When they reached the forks of the Fraser River they didn't know which fork to take—the north fork, which is now the McGregor River, or the south fork. They puzzled for a time before deciding to take the south fork, which led them on through the

The B.C. Express
Passing through the
Grand Canyon B.C.

With its engine in full reverse, the steamer *BC Express* approached Green's Rock, while the off-loaded passengers walked around the upper canyon on the portage trail, c. 1912. BC ARCHIVES A-08049

Yellowhead Pass to Edmonton. These four men—T.M. Love, Thomas Clover, Alfred Perry and D.F. McLaurin—had in their possession $1,600 worth of gold (about $80,000 in today's currency). They are believed to be the only gold seekers to travel east to the Prairies and may well have helped instigate the Overlanders' trip two years later.

The first recorded drowning in the Grand Canyon appears to have been one of the Overlanders, a group of immigrants who came across Canada in 1862. Tempted by the gold strikes along the Fraser River and the mystical land called the Cariboo, these courageous adventurers went through months of abject misery. After an incredibly tough and hazardous journey of about three months' duration, they crossed the Prairies until they reached the head of the Fraser River. They followed it for many miles until they reached a spot where they split into two groups. One group headed overland along the North Thompson River while the other party, under the command of Captain McMicking, decided to float down the Fraser River. After constructing a main raft twenty by eighty feet (6 x 24 m) in size, and several rafts that measured twenty by forty feet (6 x 12 m), they set off on their journey. To save time they installed fireplaces of rock and clay so that they wouldn't have to stop the rafts in order to cook. As a means of determining what dangers lay ahead, they fashioned many dugout canoes from cottonwood trees; these canoes were to act as scouts to check the river ahead of the rafts.

In his book *The Fraser*, Bruce Hutchison wrote, "The Fraser, long accustomed to men's folly, was carrying that day a cargo of lunacy and illusion without equal on the rivers of America."

At the edge of starvation after nearly three months on the trail, these people eventually exhausted their food supply and were forced to feed on chipmunks, birds, porcupines and even skunks. Their hopes of finding big-game animals along the river were in vain. As others that came along the river in the early years discovered, there was little in the way of big game except for caribou higher up in the mountains.

They had been led to believe that the Fraser River would peacefully float them down to the gold fields, so the Overlanders drifted downriver from first light until dark. Thinking that the river route was not dangerous, they were completely unprepared for what awaited them in the Grand Canyon.

The first canoe, carrying three men from Toronto, reached the canyon two days ahead of the first raft. They beached and began lowering the canoe into the rapids with a rope; the canoe bobbed for a moment before it was sucked down and swept away. Left without food or shelter, one of the men—Pattison—was near death by the time the first raft arrived. Three other men tied two canoes together; at the first riffle they capsized and a man named Robertson drowned. In total, ten canoes were lost at this spot.

As the *Queenston* approached the canyon, almost all of the crew had fallen asleep, and they were almost in the rapids before they were aware of it. Captain McMicking wrote that at half past five on Saturday morning, September 6, they were startled by a loud roaring noise that broke the silence of the morning, the source of which was soon explained when the lookout shouted, "Breakers ahead!" They had reached the big canyon and were already being swept toward the top rapids so quickly that they barely had time to row ashore and tie up the raft before they were drawn in.

After landing they went some distance along the shore to examine the place before attempting the run. They found that the rapids consisted of three distinct stretches with small bays or eddies of quiet water between them. The banks on both sides were very rocky and precipitous and the channel, which was narrow and obstructed in

Living on a scow. COURTESY VIOLET BAXTER

many places by pointed rocks, contained six sharp angles through which the water poured. They didn't like the idea of risking their lives in this perilous place, but there was no alternative; it was either go through the rapids or die of starvation where they were.

They found a way to portage their supplies around the first two stretches of wild water but were unable to portage around the rocky bluffs of the third because of the sheer rock walls. After leaving their supplies and ten men on the raft, the rest positioned themselves along the steep bank where they planned to help if possible. Finally the raft was pushed off and went tearing into what one described as "the very jaws of death." Before them on the right rose a rocky reef against which the water whipped itself into foam, and on the other side was a seething whirlpool waiting to drown any person within its reach. Gathering great speed, they rushed toward the rock, where tragedy seemed imminent. McMicking wrote:

> Not a word was spoken except the necessary orders of the pilot, which were distinctly heard on shore above all the commotion. Now was the critical moment. With everyone working the oars, the raft shot closely past the rock, tearing away the stern rowlock, and glided safely down into the eddy below.

The second raft to appear at the canyon was the *Huntington*, whose crew members had no way of knowing if the *Queenston* had survived. They sized it up and, like the group before them, made most of the men walk around the portage while eight drove the raft through. Mr. Fortune wrote in his diary:

> We pushed off and then kept working our sweeps to prevent going to the right side. Down we shot like a cork—a whirl caught the left forward corner of the raft, holding it fast while another terrific eddy below the great rock caught the right after corner of the raft and thus we were anchored for a short time. Although we laboured and strained at our sweeps with two men at each handle, we failed to gain upon the power of the eddy. We were tired and troubled in this dilemma when

all of a sudden, by some freak of the eddy, we were hoisted past all danger.

By some miracle all the rafts survived the Grand Canyon and their crews made it safely to Fort George, where the weakened Pattison, however, lost his fight for life.

Back upriver, another group of stragglers reached the Grand Canyon, where seven men were again spilled into the treacherous waters and a man named Phillip Leader drowned.

All through the month of September stragglers kept coming downriver until five men arrived at the canyon—two in one canoe, and three in the other two canoes, which were lashed together. The three men in the double canoe were Carpenter, Jones and Alexander. After they had portaged the upper canyon, Carpenter went ahead to scout the area and then decided to run the lower rapids. Before returning to his friends, he took out his notebook and wrote in it for a moment. The others saw him put the note into the pocket of his coat, which he hung on a tree branch.

After leaving Jones on shore to walk around the canyon, they pushed off. What happened next is described in Alexander's diary:

> As we thought it rather dangerous, I took off my boots and buckskin shirt before we started. Then we pushed off, and went at a tremendous rate for a while, when we got among some big waves and the canoe filled over the stern and went down. When it came to the surface again Carpenter was holding to the stern and I to the bow. Then I let go and swam for it. Carpenter I never saw again, or yet the canoe. I was carried a long way under water by the undercurrent but I kept thinking that it was not all up yet and resolutely kept my mouth shut till I came to the surface and got another gulp of air, and down I went again. Sometimes I was so long under water that I could scarcely hold my breath.
>
> At last I got down out of the boiling surf and the water, though boiling, was smooth. I then began to keep myself better afloat and began to swim for shore. At first I was under water so much that all my exertions had been to keep my

head above water. I was so exhausted that I had to swim on my back and lay gasping for breath, but I was quite cool all the time (the water was remarkably cold) and managed to pull my shirt up out of my pants so as to let the water out. I had on heavy Canadian cloth pants.

After swimming a distance of about three-quarters of a mile, I touched shore but was so benumbed with the cold I could not hold on to it but drifted off again. Soon, however, I made the shore again and dug my hands among the pebbles and pulled myself out of the water and lay there.

Incredibly, Alexander had successfully swum the lower canyon, a near-impossible feat. His ordeal was not yet over, however, as he was now trapped on an island. His choice was simple—swim to the shore or starve where he lay. Alexander's diary continued:

After running about to try to warm myself a little, I jumped into the water again and swam across. Before swimming the second time I stripped off the remainder of my clothes and left them there. I was so cold that I could not close my fingers and had to swim with my hand open. Oh, I never knew what it was to be thankful to God before as when I trotted up that bank, and ever since in all my troubles and dangers I have been able to place more dependence on Him and leave all to His good pleasure.

Alexander was pulled ashore by two strangers (probably Overlanders who had caught up with the advance parties) and Jones, who had scrambled around the canyon ahead of his two friends and positioned himself to offer help.

The next day, after realizing that Carpenter had drowned, Alexander walked back around the canyon to get his shirt and boots as well as the coat that Carpenter had hung in the tree, which he needed to keep warm. He found the coat, put it on and then remembered the note Carpenter had written. He took it from the pocket and read, "Arrived this day at the Canyon at 10 a.m. and drowned running the canoe down. God keep my poor wife!"

Alexander's group was by no means the last of the Overlanders to come through the canyon. In the book *John Giscome's Country* by Bruce Ramsey, a story is told about five men—Gilbert, Thomas and William Rennie, along with John Helstone and John Wright—who attempted to run the canyon. They struck a rock and became marooned on the sandbar between the upper and lower canyons.

One month later, Gilbert and Thomas Rennie arrived at Fort George. Thomas Charles, who was in charge of the fort, sent two Natives to search for the other three men. The search was supposedly aborted, but a year later it was learned that the two Natives had actually found the missing men and made a gruesome discovery. Helstone and Wright had apparently killed William Rennie and consumed his body. The Natives had in turn killed the two cannibals, whose bodies were later found and buried by John Giscome, of Giscome Portage fame. Mr. Giscome supposedly sent a letter to Victoria attesting to this story.

Someone once said, "Time twists things" and it certainly appears

The lower canyon at peace in the low water of April. Alexander's Island is at the centre. COURTESY ELARRY EVASIN

to apply in this case, because on December 24, 1913, the following article was reprinted and carried in the *Herald:*

FIFTY YEARS AGO

A fearful tragedy from Mr. Giscome, who has just arrived from the mouth of the Quesnelle River. We learn that three miners set out from Fort George about a year ago and not returning in the spring of this year, a party went out to look for them. They discovered the tent and canoe, but everything else was gone, stolen by the Indians. It was also learned from the Indians that the men had died of starvation and that two of them had killed one of the party named Rennie, and had eaten him, leaving nothing but the skull and bones.

This version of the story caused a great deal of confusion, because it appeared to state that the incident took place near Quesnelle (re-named Quesnel after 1900). A careful read of the article shows that Mr. Giscome just arrived from Quesnel and described an incident that occurred a year earlier. I believe this was the origin of the story that had the men starting from Fort George instead of attempting to reach it.

A different version of this story, published in Bruce Hutchison's *The Fraser*, has it that at least three of the men tried to run the Grand Canyon with the result that their canoes or rafts were swamped and they became trapped on the sandbar below the upper rapids. The following summer their bodies were discovered, all torn and devoured except one, which was fully clothed and untouched. Since it seemed that no animal could reach this spot, the obvious was suspected. Fortunately, their identities were unknown and the rumours of cannibalism died with them.

This is the story I repeatedly heard as a youngster, but even this version leaves something to be desired. The suggestion that no animal could reach that spot is nonsense because the animals could easily get there after the river froze over.

There are at least five different versions of this tale, including the one in John "Jack" Pinkerton's life story. Jack spent many years prospecting and mining the Barkerville area, and Pinkerton Lake was later named after him. But though he was on the McMicking raft that made it safely to Quesnel, he was of little help; he had only heard of the disaster after the fact.

Father A.G. Morice presents another version of this cannibal story in *The History of the Northern Interior of British Columbia:*

A fourth and somewhat later party met with such a tragic fate that its bitter experiences seem to have deterred others from

The upper canyon with Cannibal Bar in the foreground. Note that the bar is devoid of driftwood. Courtesy Elarry Evasin

following in its wake. It consisted of only five Canadians, namely, three brothers called Rennie, and two men known respectively as Helstone and Wright, who simply repaired to Tête Jaune Cache, where they bought two canoes for their trip down the Fraser. With a view to greater security while shooting the rapids, they lashed these together, with the result—which would have been easily foreseen by less inexperienced boatmen—that their craft, becoming unmanageable in the midst of the raging waters of the torrent, was swamped, with the loss of most of their property. None but two of the Rennie brothers could swim ashore, while the other three men reached a rock in the middle of the stream, where they remained for two days and two nights without a morsel of food and suffering severely from the cold of the opening winter.

When they were at length hauled over by the means of a rope thrown to them from the shore, they were so frostbitten and exhausted that they could proceed no farther; which seeing, the two Rennies, who had already spent two days in working out their release from their narrow prison, provided them with a quantity of firewood, and, having parted in their favour with almost all that remained of their scanty provisions, they set out on foot to seek assistance at Fort George, which was not very far distant. But so little inured were these men to the hardships incident to the wilds of New Caledonia that it took them twenty-eight days to cover a distance which they had expected to traverse in six, and which an Indian could easily make in three.

Natives were then dispatched from Fort George to lend assistance to the unfortunates left behind, who were expected to have slowly followed the two Rennie brothers, after recuperating a little from their terrible experience on the lonely rock in the Fraser. But the Indians soon returned, alleging the depth of the snow as an excuse for the failure of their journey.

Other Indians, however, discovered the party sometime afterwards. Helstone and Wright were still alive, but, maddened by hunger, had killed Rennie. When they were found, they had eaten all but his legs, which they held in their hands at the time. They were covered with blood, being engaged in tearing the raw flesh from the bones with their teeth. The Indians attempted to light a fire for them, when the two cannibals drew their revolvers, and looked so wild and savage that the Indians fled and left them to their fate, not daring to return.

The following spring a party of miners, on their way to Peace River, were guided by Indians to the place where these men were seen by them. The bones of two were found piled in a heap; one skull had been split open by an axe, and many of the other bones showed the marks of teeth. The third was missing, but was afterwards discovered a few hundred yards from the camp. The skull had been cloven by an axe, and the clothes stripped from the body, which was little decomposed.

The interpretation of these signs could hardly be mistaken. The last survivor had killed his fellow murderer and eaten him, as shown by the gnawed bones so carefully piled in as heap. He had, in turn, probably been murdered by Indians, for the principal part of the dead men's property was found in their possession.

The foregoing story is identical to what must be the original version, taken from Milton and Cheadle's *The Northwest Passage by Land*.

Take note that Gilbert and Rennie headed for Fort George, which was not very far distant. To me this indicates plainly that they were upriver of Fort George, as they would have headed for Quesnel if they were farther downriver, or at least they would have known how far it was back to Fort George. As it turned out, they didn't know how far it was to Fort George and that is why it took them so long to get there. It is also my belief that these men were trapped on the sandbar between the two sets of rapids in the Grand Canyon upriver of Fort George. The two men—Gilbert and Rennie—walked around the canyon so they escaped. Unable to swim or build a raft, the other three men had no possibility of escape and eventually turned to cannibalism before the last of them died of hypothermia as winter approached. Surely all will agree that these three men would not have camped by the river and waited to die unless they were trapped. They certainly would have continued on toward Fort George or Quesnel; therefore the version of them being trapped on the sandbar is the only one that makes sense. It must be further noted that the two survivors had to cross two rivers between the Grand Canyon and Fort George. In such a weakened condition, with no material with which to build rafts, they may have searched for days at each river before finding a place to ford the streams. As for Mr. Giscome's story that he buried the remains, this is entirely possible, as the bar would have remained exposed until the high water in June 1863.

It must also be noted that this bar is submerged during periods of high water, when driftwood runs downriver. Therefore the driftwood does not hang up on the bar. This means that there was no material with which to fashion a raft to facilitate the men's escape from the bar. The reason why the Rennie brothers did not build a raft and attempt a rescue was twofold: they didn't have any material to work with, and they were obviously aware of the second canyon immediately below the trapped men.

Whichever story is closest to the truth matters little now; the point is that these travellers went through hell. Just how many people died is unknown, but it was established that some of the Overlanders straggled so far behind that winter caught them in the mountains and they perished.

Another man who came downriver with the Overlanders was Robert Halloway, who crossed Canada to Tête Jaune in an ox cart and eventually landed in the Cariboo. After gold mining for a few years, he moved to Victoria. In 1868 he returned to Barkerville and purchased the *Cariboo Sentinel*, which was destroyed in the great fire of 1876. The printing plant was saved, however, and moved to Richfield where it operated for a short time. Then Mr. Halloway moved back to Victoria and joined the *Victoria Colonist*. He also worked for the *Standard* and the provincial government until his death at the age of seventy-five.

Of the Overlanders that did get through to Quesnellemouth

(present-day Quesnel), the two main groups arrived there on September 11 and October 4, perilously close to winter. The name Quesnellemouth was used to distinguish it from Quesnel Forks, which was sixty miles up the Quesnel River. It was changed from Quesnellemouth to Quesnelle about 1870 and then to Quesnel around 1900.

In 1864 another adventurous soul named Dr. John Rae took the hazardous trip through the Yellowhead Pass and down the Fraser River through Fort George to the Pacific coast. Dr. Rae made several trips into the Arctic and was among those who discovered the fate of the doomed Franklin Expedition.

During the winter of 1874–75, a survey party under the command of Mr. Jarvis (Jarvis Creek) and his assistant, Mr. Hannington, set out to search for a possible pass through the Rockies. This was just one of many surveys done for the Canadian Pacific Railway. These two men left Quesnelle on December 9 and stopped at Fort George, where they completed their outfitting. When the rivers were frozen solid, they set out up the Fraser River with eight men and six dog teams. They passed Giscome Portage, then left the Fraser River and followed the Big Salmon (now McGregor) River to what is now Herrick Creek.

After finding that this creek offered no pass, they returned and followed the main branch of the river to the Continental Divide, arriving there on February 24, 1875. In his book *A History of Prince George*, F.E. Runnalls wrote:

> They endured many hardships as they explored the rough mountainous area of the watersheds of the Smoky and Athabaska Rivers. They faced severe storms and low temperatures, and when they eventually reached Jasper House on March 5th, they were in an exhausted and starving condition. They were given food by friendly Indians, however, and proceeding eastward they reached St. Ann twelve days later.

Though the pass found by Mr. Jarvis and his party was never utilized, we owe them and all the other surveyors a great debt. His group was just one of many surveying parties that endured terrible hardships in the development of this great province.

Just how many surveyors travelled the upper Fraser River route is unknown to me, but in the early 1880s the railway genius Sandford Fleming journeyed through to the Pacific. As we shall see, it was this route that was later followed by the Grand Trunk Pacific Railway.

For a time after Mr. Fleming's trip the Fraser River above Fort George seemed to fade into obscurity though it is certain that trappers and prospectors moved through the area. Then in 1887 an adventurous soul named J. Turner Turner came up the Fraser River from Fort George with several Native guides. In his book, *Three Years Hunting and Trapping in America and the Great Northwest*, Mr. Turner wrote:

> On the following day, being the sixth since leaving Fort George, toward evening we reached the cañon. The water being as low as it ever is, though even in this stage it would be impossible to get a loaded canoe through; while in high water nothing would induce an Indian to attempt a passage either up or down. Whether it would be possible for a canoe to live or no, I cannot say, but the risk would be considerable. The canoes were got through as soon as possible after our arrival, and the next day the things were replaced after being packed [portaged] about half a mile.

After trapping the entire winter Mr. Turner, along with his wife and a friend named Fred, came back downriver to the canyon with his Native guides, who had returned from Fort George to assist them. These guides kept urging him to hurry because the water was rising rapidly, and the danger level with it. Mr. Turner continued:

> It was too late to get the canoes through that night, therefore as much baggage as possible was packed over, and everything set for a start at daybreak. Next morning the cat was missing and could be found nowhere. A full hour was wasted hunting for her, until the Indians declared that the rising water was rendering the cañon so dangerous that in a short time it would become impassable. Feeling like murderers at leaving

a comrade in the lurch, we were forced to abandon the poor cat, for there was more bad water below the cañon, and we dared remain no longer. We therefore started along the trail to the further end of the cañon, while the Indians lowered the canoes with long ropes past the most dangerous points, finally emerging in safety.

The great respect that the Natives had for the canyon was justified; their refusal to traverse it in high water was undoubtedly the result of lessons learned the hard way.

Canyon Memories

For several years after Mr. Turner's trip it appears that few people travelled the Grand Canyon except for the occasional prospector or trapper. One trapper was W.E. Halloway, better known as "Beaver Bill," who passed through the canyon in 1897 on his way to Tête Jaune by canoe.

The solitude of the river was about to change a great deal with the building of the Grand Trunk Pacific Railway . From 1906 through 1910 a great many surveyors worked along the upper river and they were almost totally dependent on the Natives for manning the canoes and scows that moved the crews and their equipment along the waterway.

There was an influx of settlers into the interior of BC, but the new arrivals had little or no experience with whitewater, defined at that time as water moving ten miles (16 km) per hour or faster. This put the Natives—who had travelled the rivers for countless generations—in a decided position of power. Their expertise was in constant demand and it is safe to say that the surveying of the new railway would have been delayed several years without their assistance. This dependence on the

Natives sometimes led to resentment, as shown by an article that appeared in Quesnel's *Cariboo Observer* on June 26, 1909:

> A correspondent at Fort George informs us that the Indians there can now be hired to do manual labour for $1.50 per day of 21 hours. This shows that the day of the Red-man's ill gained prosperity is now on the wane. At the time when the GTP surveys were being run through this district, the railway company had to depend for the transportation of all their supplies upon the northern Indians, and at the same period the many timber cruisers working on the northern rivers were also dependent upon Indians for canoe men; competition for their services resulted to the detriment of commerce in the North, and Indians commanded from $2.50 to $4.00 per day.

The foregoing simply amazes me. That people could be jealous of the Natives for making this amount of money in return for risking their lives defies logic. Imagine their shock when they found out what the Canyon Cats earned just a couple of years later—over ten times as much!

The expertise of the Native rivermen was well documented by early-day adventurers. Writer C. Galloway, in his book *The Call of the West*, described a trip down the Bear (now Bowron) River in 1912.

Their trip started when he met a survey party at Bear Lake, where they built three boats for the journey downriver. While they were at work on the boats a man named Mr. Pearson came back upriver to report that one of his surveyors had been drowned about thirty miles back. This obviously didn't deter the men because they finished their boats and then carried on with their trip. Mr. Galloway wrote:

> On the morning of the second day we reached the first rapids, and here our boatmen's skill showed itself. These Indians from Fort George have been born and bred on these rivers and know all there is to be known about handling a boat or canoe. In the calm places the paddles are used, but wherever the water is shallow and rapid, the poles are in requisition; it is wonderful how they will bring the boat to a standstill and

hold it in the midst of rushing water, the captain at the stern and the mate at the bow. The passenger in the middle of the boat also gives what help he can with his pole. Then when the passage has been decided upon the boat is then poled back against the stream for some distance, and diverted into the required channel.

Now and then they get out and wade, guiding the boat in the way it should go in the shallow places among the rocks; it is a masterful piece of work, the handling of a fragile boat among the turbulent waters. At one place the passengers are landed on a long island, and walk down half a mile while the boats are skillfully guided down the shallow rock-strewn channel.

At the rapids the water is boiling over the rocks; it needs a skilled boatman to see the channel and follow it. If the boat were to swing around and dash its side against a rock it would be all up within a moment. If she commences to swing around, and cannot be held by the poles, there is only one thing to do, and that is to jump out and hold her. There is no time for thought; action must be instinctive or it will be too late. That is where a novice is so utterly useless; while he wastes a second in thinking what to do, the damage is done and the boat is lost. That is undoubtedly what happened in the case of Pearson's party; most of them were men entirely unacquainted with river craft, and it is not surprising that they had several mishaps, fortunately without loss of life except in that one case.

But, thanks to our expert boatmen, we get through with no mishap, and presently we find ourselves in a deep, dark canyon where the water is black and deep. And just below the other party is encamped, for in this pool lies that poor fellow's body.

The foregoing is just one of countless stories that illustrate the skill of these Native rivermen.

By 1909 the prospect of the GTP Railway had brought a flood of people into the interior of BC. Many came downriver on scows, as well as by raft and canoe. In spite of the numerous drowning accidents reported in eastern newspapers, people and supplies kept coming. The result was that between 1909 and 1913, thousands of vessels made their way into the Grand Canyon, often with disastrous results. The newspapers of the time frequently reported the discovery of unidentifiable corpses floating along the Fraser River.

As tough and dangerous as it was to come downriver, surveyors had the near-impossible task of taking canoes and scows loaded with supplies against the river current. This meant they had to portage all their supplies and then line their river craft through the canyons and rapids.

Possibly the most startling change ever to occur at the Grand Canyon was the arrival of the small sternwheeler *Nechacco*. In October 1909 it entered the canyon. By means of three rings placed on the canyon walls, Captain Bonser lined his steamer through the upper rapids, which until that time had been considered an impassable barrier to steamers. It was hazardous work running out this line by boat from the steamers, as it had to be moved three times before calm water was reached above the rapids. More than one life was lost in these manoeuvres during the next four years, but on that occasion the little *Nechacco* made it through without a hitch.

At about the same time that Captain Bonser took the little steamer through the canyon, a reporter visited and took several pictures of the area. He noted that there were two sets of falls in the upper canyon, each about two feet high. He also stated, "We do not believe that the canyon can be made navigable for its entire length, but should the Dominion Government decide ever to turn their attention to that place, much could be done to improve the passage for canoes and scows."

This reporter thought the canyon would never be bested by steamers; he was just one of many who seriously underestimated the skill and nerve of the steamer captains.

During the winter of 1909–1910, a man named Emmet Baxter "Shorty" Haynes travelled 150 miles through the canyon by dog team delivering mail to surveyors along the upper river. It must have been a difficult mission, but it may well be that he only managed to get through during late winter after the snow settled or the river became windswept, allowing easy travel for his dog team.

An incident in 1909 demonstrates what the surveyors were up against. Three men named F. Fetterly, S. Mallock and C. Shepherd left Quesnel on July 15 for Tête Jaune Cache to complete a survey of the upper Fraser River. Ten days later they lost their canoe and four hundred dollars (twenty thousand dollars in today's value) worth of provisions in the Grand Canyon. Fortunately all the men managed to survive and return to Fort George.

Almost as if the mail delivery through the canyon heralded the opening up of the area, a second sternwheeler visited the canyon in 1910. This was the small steamer *Fort Fraser*, which passed through on its way to Tête Jaune. However, due to low water levels, it was forced to drop its load of supplies well short of its destination.

One regular visitor to the canyon was George Williams, who became known as the "Wizard of the River." Born in Kansas, George Williams came to Canada in 1905, where he became a mule-skinner— or muleteer as they were often referred to—for the famed packer Cataline. In 1906 he came to the Fort George area, where he hired out with the Grand Trunk Pacific Railway survey crews and worked his way west to Hazelton. There he gained proficiency on wild water by working along the Skeena hauling mail by canoe. The following year he began running the Fraser River, freighting surveyors and supplies in canoes and scows.

In 1909 George Williams took up residence in Fort George, where he went to work for the main railway contractors Foley, Welch and

Emmet Baxter "Shorty" Haynes on the right. Torpy River, c. 1920. Courtesy Jim Chambers

Stewart (FW&S)—often jokingly referred to as Frig'em, Work'em & Starv'em. It didn't take Mr. Williams very long to recognize the ability of the Native rivermen, and he quickly hired four of them on as his crewmen.

In June 1910 Mr. Williams was ordered to take a forty-two-foot dugout canoe, owned by the Hudson's Bay Company, from Fort George to Tête Jaune. The purpose of this 315-mile [507-km] journey was to pick up a man named Stanley Washburn. In his book, *Trails, Trappers and Tenderfeet*, Mr. Washburn describes his journey through the Grand Canyon. He tells how a Native called Pius took the canoe down though the upper rapids, at which point they reloaded all their supplies and carried on. Describing the lower rapids, Mr. Washburn stated:

> This place, too, had a curve in it, and I should say the current was going fully fifteen miles an hour. For a moment we hung at the entrance, and then the current caught us with the suddenness with which a piece of machinery starts when the belt is suddenly thrown on. I don't suppose the distance through this defile exceeds a mile or so, and we were through it in a few minutes, but it was certainly a boily, tumbly place while it lasted.
>
> The great danger, and in fact the only one, is from the boils and eddies created by the vast quantity of water surging through the narrow crack. Every instant a great vortex would form, sucking the water down into great eddies fifteen or twenty feet deep and eight or ten feet across at the top. The next moment these would fill and the water, in a whirling mass, would be forced three or four feet above the surface in a great "boil" as it is called out there . . .

After completing this trip, Mr. Williams, along with his expert Native rivermen, returned to Tête Jaune in two dugout canoes. This time he picked up an author named Fred Talbot. In his book *The New Garden of Canada* Mr. Talbot describes their encounter with the canyon and points out the courage and skill of the Natives who manned the canoes. He also describes what it was like to narrowly escape death in that place.

Prior to portaging around the upper rapids, the Natives handed their watches to him for safekeeping as they realized that they could get dunked running the canoes down. After doing so, the two canoes—which had been tied together—were uncoupled and the two Natives started out, one in each canoe. Mr. Talbot wrote:

The mouth of the cañon is certainly forbidding. It is not more than thirty feet across at the entrance, and the whole waters of the river, suddenly narrowed down from about 200 feet wide, have to pour through this gorge. They curl over the brink, and when the canoe dipped, half its length was out of water. Moreover, the defile twists and turns, is a mass of evil rocks, and, dropping a matter of feet in half a mile, the stream rushes through with terrific fury. It was raining hard, the sky was overladen, and the grayness of the clouds deadened the green verdure of the primeval forest on either side. Immediately below the cañon was a huge devil's bowl, the water fussing, spluttering and jumping in all directions.

Presently there was a weird shout, and the first canoe shot round the corner. The foremost Indian was standing up working like a Trojan, while the steersman had literally thrown himself on his paddle to force the boat around. In an instant he had changed his position, and, with his foot against the rim of the dugout to secure leverage, had squatted and was pulling on the paddle like grim death. The front Indian rowing as if demented, and giving vent to fierce cries of "Hudson's Bay" with each pull. They flew through the bottom portal like a flash into a big basin, almost like a lake, which was quite calm, pulled the boat round and paddled into the bank as if shooting the fiendish waters were a mere nothing. The other canoe followed hard on their heels. Both men and boats showed traces of the ordeal. The Indians were puffing like labouring locomotives after their exertion, were doused with water, and the boat itself was nearly half full.

After they safely descended the upper rapids, they tied the canoes together and then reloaded the supplies with the intent of crossing the river to portage the bottom rapids. Mr. Talbot continued:

We started off, but the Indians, finding the going easier than they expected, and plenty of water, did not land us on the opposite bank as arranged, but struck boldly for the cañon. As we slipped over the brink between the imposing cliffs, the boat suddenly awoke to life as it was caught by the rushing waters. The Indians and those of the party equipped with oars jumped to their feet, while the rest of us were ready with various articles for bailing out any water that may be shipped. About half-way through, the river turns sharply at right angles, a buttress of rock thrusting its nose half-way across the channel, around which the water swirls in a big eddy. We had reached the turn, and with a tremendous stroke Williams shouted "Now then, pull like blazes!"

Seven paddles dipped simultaneously; the tremendous leverage exerted lifted the boat half out of the water and turned her round as if on a pivot to negotiate the bend. We shipped a big wave and were bailing for dear life, since the gunwale was

George Williams and Native canoemen. Writer Fred Talbot is on the left, 1910.
COURTESY OLIVE WILLIAMS

83

almost awash. A mighty roar broke on our ears as we rounded the rock. We were on the edge of a big whirlpool where the water was swinging round at terrific speed and with a vortex some six feet deep, like a big cup, the bottom of which we could plainly see as a mass of foam. The canoes had struck the edge of the whirlpool, and we were being sucked in. The men rowed harder than ever, the two steersmen hanging over the canoes as they pushed against their oars to force the prow of the canoe away from the maelstrom. They had to dig their fingernails into their sweeps to retain their hold, as they could feel the whirlpool tugging at the submerged blades. If one snapped, the Grand Cañon would have "fixed" another party. But the paddles held, and as the nose of the catamaran was slowly and almost imperceptibly jammed round, the outer swirl caught the stern of the canoe and flung it with an unseating jerk across the river clear of the peril.

Immediately after they were clear of the whirlpool, the Natives gave a derisive laugh, almost as if they were mocking the river. Many other early-day travellers along the rivers have described this same thing: while in peril, the Natives would shout "Hudson's Bay! Hudson's Bay!" but the minute they succeeded in escaping dangerous canyons or rapids they would break into uncontrollable laughter. Perhaps this was their way of expressing joy at having cheated death once again.

One must also take note that it was raining hard when Talbot's party reached the canyon. As in the case of the Overlanders, when it rained day after day, the water level rose and the canyon turned into an evil monster.

After the completion of this trip, Mr. Talbot wrote yet another book, *The Making of a Great Canadian Railway*, in which he describes very well the hardships and dangers faced by the early surveyors who laid out the grade. He also tells of the courageous rivermen who drowned while attempting to supply the surveyors' camps upriver of Fort George. This often meant taking supply-laden dugout canoes or scows hundreds of miles against the river current.

After describing the Giscome Rapids, Mr. Talbot goes on, " . . . Some sixty miles beyond is the Grand Canyon of the upper Fraser, which is a veritable death-trap, where the inexpert, as well as the dexterous water-dog [experienced riverman] often has met his end. Even the Indians for the most part regard it with awe, especially during certain times of the year when it is little better than a maelstrom, and wherein several members of their tribe have met their Waterloo . . ."

Many of the people employed in this dangerous supply work were Natives, who, as already pointed out, were expert rivermen. Because they travelled by canoe, the only trails they made were around canyons or dangerous rapids. Therefore packing with horses would have meant months of trail-cutting along the riverbanks. For this reason the men taking supplies to the early upriver survey camps were forced to "run the river"—often with disastrous results.

Mr. Talbot described a supply-laden canoe being lined up the rapids:

> . . . It was a heavy craft, and the Indians were hauling might and main, but making slow headway. Suddenly there was a sharp cry from the man in the boat. The curling water had swept the pole out of his hand, and the canoe, deprived of its guiding influence, was swung round by the rushing water and hurled with terrific force against a rock. The boat split in two from end to end, as if cleft with an axe; the rope broke, and cargo, wreck of canoe, and Indian were thrown into the water. The Indian was never seen again.
>
> In another instance a party was coming up through the same rapids, and all were poling vigorously as the craft was otherwise untrammeled. But the water was running more swiftly than the canoe-men, including members of a survey party had intimated, and for their error of judgment they paid dearly. The canoe was tossed against a half-submerged rock, and in the manner of the dugout that is fashioned from the brittle cottonwood, it succumbed to the impact. In a few moments the occupants were engaged in a desperate struggle for their lives in the foaming water. One man was caught by the undertow and never reappeared; two others failed to gain the shore and were drowned, while three were rescued . . .

Aside from the many people that were drowned in 1910, there were some other strange happenings that unfolded at the canyon. One such event occurred when a man named Bowman passed through. He had built a canoe at Tête Jaune and was heading to Fort George and then on to Bella Coola. What made this trip so unusual was the fact that Bowman only had one arm and was travelling alone. It is interesting to note that he successfully completed his trip!

An unfortunate accident that took place in the Giscome Rapids sixty kilometres upriver of Fort George had a surprise ending. A scow-load of flour was being moved through the rapids when it struck a rock and was torn apart. Octogenarian Carl Strom of Prince George recalls hearing this story many times in his youth. The surprising part is that the scow and flour were recovered during low water that same fall and the flour was still good. The outside two inches of the load was hard but it had sealed and protected the inner flour, which was still edible.

A rather humorous story unfolded when George Williams and a friend named John Fountain were on their way downriver from Tête Jaune Cache. Two days earlier a daring young man had left the Cache on a raft, so George and John expected to catch up to him in their canoe. They came around a bend in the river to witness an unbelievable scene. The raft rider—a man named Pat Carigan—was sitting

George Williams moves the second dugout canoe up through the Grand Canyon assisted by Fort George Natives, 1910. Courtesy Olive Williams

up in a partly submerged tree singing "Ireland Was Ireland When England Was a Pup."

George and John picked the hapless fellow off his perch and took him ashore, where they made a fire and got some warmth back into his body. They learned that his raft had struck the tree the previous day and had come apart from the impact. Pat had spent the night in the tree, sopping wet, and had almost perished from the cold. Despite the terrible condition he was in, he was still singing songs when his rescuers arrived.

In 1911 a man named Alan Bouchier brought a scow upstream from Fort George, heading upriver for Tête Jaune. Aboard was eight tons of merchandise needed to open a store at Tête Jaune. All these supplies had to be portaged around the canyons and rapids—an incredible undertaking—but the crew of four white men and three Natives completed the 507-kilometre trip in thirty-two days, arriving at their destination just as the river froze over for the winter.

Bouchier's scow was just one of many that made the hazardous upriver journey during those years. Many of these rivermen were lost in those early years, heroes that will forever remain unknown.

Alan Bouchier was a jack of all trades, in that he was a qualified riverman, a merchant and a magistrate at Tête Jaune for a time. During his time as magistrate, he sent an average of six bootleggers a month to Kamloops, where most were sentenced to six months in prison.

As if nature wasn't doing enough damage to the newcomers descending on the Fort George area, the following article describes just one of several suicides that occurred around Fort George. It depicts just how tough things were at the time and how some were unable to cope:

A man named H.P. Newcombe, hailing from Falmouth, Mass., who arrived here lately, committed suicide by filling his pockets with rocks and jumping into the river at the foot of Fourth Street on Wednesday evening at 6 o'clock. Newcombe had been acting strangely for some time and was under police surveillance. Immediately preceding the act of suicide he had gone to the door of the Hotel Northern dining room and

Entrepreneur Alan Bouchier. Courtesy Violet Baxter

finding it full he walked down to the river. The constable followed him and seeing him, Newcombe motioned him away and leaping onto a large rock, sprang into the Fraser. He sank immediately but came to the surface twice afterwards and was apparently struggling desperately to regain the shore. William [Billy] Seymour, an Indian, went to the rescue but the suicide did not reappear . . .

Newcombe's body was found a short time later several miles south of Quesnel at a woodcutter's camp. He was one of four men known to have filled their pockets with rocks and jumped or waded out into the river to their deaths.

The woodcutter's camp mentioned previously was just one of many that dotted the riverbanks during the years of steamer operations. The steamers needed a mountain of firewood to climb the mighty Fraser, especially when they ploughed through rapids and canyons. According to records kept by one of the large steamers, these firewood depots were placed between ten and fifteen miles apart along the river, depending on the speed of the current. Each steamer burned between two and five cords of wood per hour depending on the size of the ship and the speed of the water. Obviously they used much more wood going against the current than when they were travelling

Steamer *Fort Fraser* wooding up at Giscome Portage, 1910. COURTESY VIOLET BAXTER

downstream. One passenger on a steamer noted that when the passengers assisted the crew, it only took ten minutes to load four cords of wood on board and get underway.

By 1911 the railway reached Tête Jaune, with the result that a great many men were contracted to bring loaded scows downriver to Fort George. This involved an enormous undertaking, in that it took two to three weeks in high water to paddle the dugout canoes upstream to Tête Jaune. Then it took at least a week to cut timbers and build a scow. When the hazardous journey to Fort George was accomplished the round trip started over again. This meant a maximum of four trips per year.

Without question the main cause of tragedy along the waterway was the rocks that lurked near the surface of the river. The first record I found of expenditures for rock removal was in 1908, when about twenty thousand dollars was spent in Cottonwood Canyon, 120 kilometres downriver from Fort George. The net result was a media claim of blatant political patronage. The *Herald* noted:

> This sort of work did not result in the cleaning up of the river, and in many instances the appropriations were squandered without material results. This was particularly evident in the Cottonwood Canyon, 20 miles north of Quesnel, where an

TENDERS WANTED

TENDERS will be received by the undersigned until further notice for the cutting of cordwood at points between South Fort George and Tête Jaune Cache.

Wood to be piled on the riverbank at places readily accessible at any stage of the water. Fir wood to be cut in localities where procurable.

Thomas Chetwynd
Local agent,
BRITISH COLUMBIA EXPRESS COMPANY.

This advertisement for woodcutters was taken from the *Herald* newspaper dated December 9, 1911.

expenditure of about $20,000 was made in 1908, with the net result of a trail round the rock walls of the canyon, which ate up most of the money and was of very little use, and a few rocks were blown from the channel.

During the winter of 1909 some money had been spent at Fort George Canyon. Quesnel's *Cariboo Observer* saw it this way:

A Dominion Government river foreman named J. [Fred] Hedon arrived here from Revelstoke on Wednesday last to commence work upon the clearing of the obstructions from the Fort George Canyon. A small appropriation has already been made for the work, which, we understand, will begin as soon as the stage of the water will permit. Fort George Canyon is located about 15 miles below Fort George on the Fraser River. The canyon proper is divided into three channels by two high islands of rock, of these channels the eastern is at present impassable to navigation on the upstream journey, as a submerged reef causes a fall of several feet in the fairway, this channel is navigated however by steamboats running with the current, though the undertaking is a risky one.

The centre channel is impassable, owing to its shallowness whilst the western channel, known as the slough, is a narrow backwater through which the steamboats pass upstream at present. Authorities claim that the blowing out of the reef in the eastern channel would cause much of the water to divert from the centre and western channels, therefore increasing the water volume and strength of the current throughout the length of the steamboat channel, as above the islands the eastern channel is the main channel, which is divided by the islands and reefs. No doubt a great deal can be done to render the Fort George Canyon more easily navigable, but the peculiar formation of the place will offer many difficulties. Mr. Hedon has had much experience in this class of work and is already known in this section as he assisted in the clearing of the Cottonwood Canyon last year. That canyon is now easily navigated.

One can't help but note that the two newspapers are in direct contradiction, the Quesnel paper stating that the previous year's blasting had been successful. It appears the real issue was which political party one favoured. As for the blasting results at Fort George Canyon, the *Fort George Tribune* stated on October 16:

> Charles Leanard, one of the men employed at Fort George Canyon in improving the channel of the river, was in Fort George on election day en route to Quesnel, where he lives. He may be quoted as saying that, for the amount of money spent ($2,500), good work was done. The rocks in the slough on the west side of the river were removed, so as to make a navigable channel in high water. In low water the channel now used will have to do; but the projecting ends of several rocks were blown off, which will help a little. Anchor bolts and rings were put in four places in the slough, so that lines may be used in going both up and downstream. The work was done under Mr. Hedon of Revelstoke.

Was the blasting successful? We only have to read on to see that there were more steamer disasters in the Fort George Canyon than in all the other canyons and rapids on the Fraser River combined.

Small amounts of money continued to be spent on blasting from time to time, but not enough to remove the worst obstacles. In an effort to cut down on the human and material losses, the Federal Department of Works finally took action. The story was carried in the *Herald* of September 9, 1911:

> Fred Hedon, in the employ of the Federal Department of Works, arrived here this week to clear the eastern channel in the Fort George Canyon of obstructions to navigation. The Dominion Government has appropriated the sum of $8,000 for the work. The eastern channel of the canyon is the main waterway. It is dangerous to navigation owing to a reef of rock that extends almost entirely across it from the shore to a large rock island near the southern end of the canyon. This reef, we understand, is to be blown out. Other appropriations are

to be spent on work in the Nechako River very shortly. We have heard nothing of appropriations for work in the Grand Canyon, or in the Giscome Rapids, both of which places need attention to render the river properly navigable between here and Tête Jaune Cache. In the opinion of Captain Foster the

Bob Dondale and author Jack Boudreau examine a small anchor bolt used to lower scows, rafts and canoes down through a canyon.

Grand Canyon could be made navigable, without serious danger to steamboats, by the expenditure of a very small sum. Capt. Foster took the steamer *Chilcotin* through the lower Grand Canyon this week. He informs us that the canyon is "a good steam-boating proposition." In his estimation Giscome Rapids need attention badly. These rapids are full of boulders, and in any stage of the water, excepting when the river is high, it is only with great difficulty that a large steamboat can navigate the rapids. This could be remedied by blowing out the boulders that obstruct the best channel.

During the following winter Hedon and his crew spent the allotment and the obstructing reef was partially blown away. Many people suggested that the money had been wasted and, judging by the great number of steamer accidents that took place in this canyon during the following years, they were probably correct.

Finally the main railway contractors—FW&S—took matters into their own hands by hiring a powder expert named Frank Freeman to deal with the obstructions in the upper canyons and rapids. By 1912 Frank had completed his task of blasting out the railway right-of-way between Fort George and Fort Fraser, so he came down the Fraser River from Tête Jaune, blasting the worst rocks and logjams along the

Surveyors lining a dugout canoe over a set of falls, c.1909. COURTESY OLIVE WILLIAMS

way. Finally he entered the Grand Canyon with a crew of men and began blowing out the rocks that had been such a threat to the steamers and scows. Known as the "River Hog," Frank succeeded in blasting a channel through which the steamers could move in safety. The fact that no serious steamer incidents occurred in this most dangerous canyon attests to the skill and knowledge of this man.

When Frank's men finished their work at the Grand Canyon, it was noticed that the two small sets of falls in the upper rapids had disappeared. This caused the water to speed up considerably, and made it more difficult for the sternwheelers to climb the upper canyon. Rings had been fastened to the canyon walls, and by the use of a capstan the steamers were able to winch themselves up the rapids. And so, while the danger from boulders was abated somewhat, the increased water speed led to a continuing loss of life, especially among the scow and raft pilots, many of whom met their fate at Green's Rock, the most dangerous place in the upper rapids. This big rock stuck out from shore just around a sharp bend, and from the moment it came into view there were only a few precious seconds of time to move the scow out of danger.

Perhaps because of this great loss of men and material, a group of men under Joe McNeil took up residence at the canyon. Called Canyon Cats, they saw a golden opportunity to make a fortune running scows, rafts and boats through the canyon. All that was needed was an abundance of courage and a willingness to study the river and learn to read the water.

They started out charging a minimum of $10 to run a scow through the canyon—no easy task when some of them were loaded down with up to forty tons of supplies. This meant that if four men were required to handle the scow, they received the princely sum of $2.50 each for risking their lives. It didn't take these Canyon Cats very long to realize that they could charge much more, and that is exactly what they did. Once they had moved a raft or scow safely through, they would scamper back to the head of the canyon and bargain with the next inexperienced pilot who could afford their services.

Generally speaking, scow pilots were those who ran the scows along the river and may or may not have guided them through the canyon. These pilots earned between $5 and $10 per day, depending on their experience and skill. Since workmen on the adjacent grade were being paid $2 to $3.50 per day, the pilots appeared to be well paid. But it was the Canyon Cats who really cashed in. Several of them—such as Fred Bennett, George Booth and Norman Rooney—claimed that they each earned over $1,000 per month in 1913. This comes to about $50,000 per month in today's currency and shows that these Canyon Cats were truly an elite group. Some of the other men who worked as Canyon Cats were Charles Freeman, James Baker, Jake Smedley, A. "Sandbar Slim" Dieber, "Slim" Miller, "Slim" Cowart, Norman Scott and Joe Guay, who lived on to become a well-known camp cook throughout the interior of BC.

While commenting on the use of scows along the river in the March 1, 1913 edition of the *Herald*, the writer reminisced:

> Freighting by this means involves a considerable risk, as the handling of heavily laden scows in such water as that encountered in the Grand Canyon and the Giscome and Goat Rapids is a dangerous undertaking. The writer once took a scow-load of freight upriver through the Grand Canyon—before the days of steamboats on the upper river—with a crew of Indians. In running down the canyon with the light scow a rock was struck, which, had the scow been loaded, would certainly have wrecked the outfit.

Mrs. Houghtaling of Prince George told the story of her encounter with the Canyon Cats when her family took a trip down the Fraser River from Tête Jaune to South Fort George in 1913.

In 1907 she and her husband Kay moved to Canada from North Dakota in a canvas-covered flatdeck truck pulled by four horses. Under the canvas was a table, a bed and a cookstove. Their two sons, four-year-old Henry and two-year-old Charles, slept on the floor, while the table was turned over to make a bed for five-year-old Gertrude. After their arrival in Edmonton they decided to follow the GTP Railway construction heading west into BC. By October 1907 they reached Stony Plains, where they spent the winter. Then it was on to Prairie Creek, where their daughter Mary was born.

They followed the railroad construction, at times running

stopping places, cafés and even a store, while Kay had four teams of horses freighting for the railway. In total, they spent a year at Mile 12, twelve miles west of the Alberta–BC Boundary, and two years at Tête Jaune where their daughter Juanita was born. This was where their greatest adventure really started.

They bought a scow forty feet by twelve feet, loaded all their possessions into it and floated downriver. Though they ran all the other rapids by themselves, they paid $100 to the Canyon Cats to have their craft safely taken through the Grand Canyon. This would be the equivalent of at least $5,000 in today's currency!

The Houghtaling family finally arrived in Fort George in October 1913, which was dangerously close to winter. With the lumber from the scow and additional lumber purchased from Peden's mill, they built a house and moved in just as the temperature dropped to -50° C.

Some of the experienced pilots refused to pay the Canyon Cats and ran their own scows through the canyon. One such man was the aforementioned George Williams. In 1965 his wife Edna reminisced, "George took on a contract freighting supplies from Tête Jaune to South Fort George for Al Johnson of the Northern Hotel, and for Billy Blair of Blair's Outfitting Company. He received $1,400 per trip for this work and if he was lucky he could make one round trip per month during the summer. He had to hire three men for the trip and build a new scow at Tête Jaune. He saved $100 a trip by running the canyon himself, so he didn't have to hire the experts."

The year was 1911. George acquired a motorized boat for transporting scows along the river during 1912–1913. Just an indication of how successful Williams was at delivering merchandise was given when Kennedy, Blair & Company in Fort George published a correction in the *Herald*, which stated that their previous statement announcing the arrival of a million pounds of merchandise was in error. It should have read "one and a quarter-million pounds."

On August 3, 1912, the *Herald* expressed its view of the loss of life along the river with the drawing that appears on the next page.

During a speech to his fellow Rotarians in 1951, this same George Williams—then a local merchant—told how the Canyon Cats would charge whatever the traffic would bear. In one instance they charged $300 to guide a tobacco-laden scow through the canyon; on board was a cargo valued at $25,000. This is equal to over $1 million in today's currency.

Williams continued, "Central British Columbia in the early 1900s was a land of hard-drinking and hard-working men of many nationalities, many of whom laughed at the perils of road and river to open

The caption under this illustration reads: "The loss of life by drowning in the waters of the Upper Fraser this summer has been appalling. Next year it will be worse. It is time the authorities took steps to cope with the situation."

a rich empire in the Canadian west and link eastern Canada by rail with a new Pacific port at Prince Rupert."

During his impromptu speech, George Williams told of some of the hardships and dangers of this exciting era when the country was overrun with construction workers, rivermen, trappers and gold seekers. As head packer and scow boss along the upper Fraser River, Mr. Williams had a grandstand seat from which to observe central BC's earliest pioneers.

They just don't seem to breed men like that anymore. In the hectic frontier days of Ashcroft, I watched the lumbering freight wagons and stagecoaches passing on the crude Cariboo Trail carrying adventurers and miners from all points of the compass, many of them lured by stories of riches waiting in the goldfields of the Quesnel and Barkerville region.

Stage and wagon drivers, their skill matching their vocabulary, drove horses fresh from the range with the aid of a single jerk line and matched each other's wits in getting their loads and passengers through to their destinations. Prominent among these was the late Al Young, who brought the first stagecoach into Fort George. Wearing thin gloves and a hat in fifty-two-below weather, Al was a prominent figure along the jolting Cariboo Trail in its heyday.

Picturesque river steamboats, some of which years later ended their days in the Cache at Prince George, carried the horses from Soda Creek to Quesnel where a wagon train led to the Blackwater River. There was no trail from this point to Fort George.

Mr. Williams was a member of crews making preliminary surveys for the Grand Trunk Pacific Railway across central BC. According to him, the first survey gangs skirted the McGregor River, but this route was abandoned in favour of the Fraser River right-of-way via Giscome.

After completion of the surveys, actual construction started and an unprecedented boom followed in the wake of the construction gangs. Money was easy to get but hard to spend—except in the gambling and bootlegging dens which mushroomed alongside and a short distance ahead of the brawling steel-layers.

Working with only picks, shovels, wheelbarrows and steam shovels, work gangs hacked out the right-of-way, laid the roadbed and steel just as fast as PGE [Pacific Great Eastern Railway] contractors are doing it today. But there were no eight-hour days in those times.

A book written by Bruce Hutchison tells how trappers and prospectors "ran" the North Thompson River in those days—undoubtedly an incredible feat. But I knew a grizzled pioneer who piloted a small boat up the North Thompson loaded with a year's supplies, trapped in the McGregor River country, and later floated south on the Fraser River in the fall.

The man referred to by Mr. Williams was Joe McNamee, one of the most outstanding woodsmen ever to work in the Interior. Old newspapers are rife with stories of him returning from the remotest parts of the wilderness after stays of a year or more. In each case he was always loaded down with at least one fine grizzly-bear hide among his furs. The *Herald* of June 20, 1914 noted:

> Joe McNamee, probably one of the oldest and best known trappers in the country, returned with his catch of furs this week after more than a year's absence on the north and south forks of the Big Salmon [McGregor] River. Among the large number of furs McNamee brought in was a very fine grizzly bear hide. Joe never misses bringing down one or more grizzlies.

George Williams described how in 1907 he met a trapper on the McGregor whose name inspired awe even among the Natives. He lived in the crudest manner, hiring Natives to lay out and build slab lean-tos every 10 miles along a 150-mile trapline. One season he came out with three hundred marten skins. Later Mr. Williams learned that this man was formerly a professor at an English university. From all the research I have done, it appears obvious to me that this man was Karl Moxley.

Another veteran of that trapline was Jack Evans, who took over Moxley's trapline in 1908 after Moxley struck it rich by staking timber. George told how Jack jerked a fifty-pound hand-sleigh through the wild bushlands along his line. Kid Carson was another trapper who scoffed at cabins and lived in the open on one of the longest traplines in the country.

Mr. Williams went on:

> Fur prices were low by present-day standards, but trapping was big business in those days. Trappers sported thick rolls after disposing of their catches but most of them were spent freely if not wisely. Many needed a grubstake in the fall when it was time to return to the fur country.
>
> When the toiling GTP gangs had cut through the foot-hills of the Rockies and pushed the steelhead to Tête Jaune Cache, 230 [right-of-way] miles east of Prince George, it initiated a new phase of man's fight to conquer the west. Foley, Welch and Stewart, main contractors for the rail-way, launched a big fleet of scows to transport supplies and equipment to advance depots along the right-of-way, uti-lizing the tortuous waters of the Fraser River. They were soon joined by the "Canyon Cats," independent scow-men who were anxious to cash in on the rich rewards of river transportation.
>
> I was among the scow bosses who pitted their wits and skill against the treacherous whirlpools, rapids and canyons. Loaded with twenty or thirty tons of freight, the clumsy but sturdy thirty-foot craft would drift with the current, guided when necessary by large "sweeps" fore and aft. When ap-proaching eddies or rocks the utmost skill and judgment was required in manipulating the sweeps, otherwise the scows would be piled onto the rocks or run aground with the ever-present danger of loss of crew and cargo.
>
> Some of the scows, their sweeps smashed or wrenched

from the hands of the "river hogs," would be whirled around in the strong eddies and sucked down until they were swamped. Others managed to get into the main current of the river and continue on their way downstream to new dangers.

The Grand Canyon with Green's Rock was the most dangerous spot in the 315-mile journey. Here quite a few unlucky or inexperienced crewmen met their fate. At some points long ropes were used to guide the scows into safe channels. Experienced crewmen would often return overland after "shooting" a canyon and guide transient scows through the boiling, rock-strewn river. Fees for this service ranged to $400 and resulted in bitter rivalry between FW&S and independent scow bosses.

Often two scows would be lashed together to prevent them from capsizing in swift water. Even these precautions did not entirely eliminate the danger, and on at least one occasion one of the boats was swamped and threatened to pull the other craft under. A quick-witted river hog slashed at the bindings with an axe and allowed the other boat to float free.

Salvaging supplies from wrecked scow in the upper canyon, c. 1913. NORTHERN BC ARCHIVES AND SPECIAL COLLECTIONS, PARKER BONNEY COLLECTION

Stranded crewmen, their boats swamped or smashed, would often continue their way downriver with the aid of a flimsy raft of logs held together by rope or baling wire.

But not all of them were that fortunate. Rocks and canyon walls were dotted with the hulks of crumpled scows, mute testimony to the fate of their crews. In the first summer's operation I had first-hand knowledge of seventeen rivermen who perished in the raging water after their boats had been lost. Certainly many more met a similar fate.

If there was one occupation frowned upon by life insurance companies in construction days it was that of a Fraser River scow-man. Death beckoned around every bend in the river, and only the water wise and the favorites of Lady Luck managed to survive.

A testament to the prowess of George Williams as a riverman is carried in the book *Bacon, Beans 'n Brave Hearts* by Russell Walker:

This picture [below] tells one of the most interesting stories dealt with in this book. It shows two cottonwood canoes held together by nailed wooden poles when travelling upstream. The two Indians in the outer canoe are Maurice, bow, and Michel, stern. The third man in that canoe and working as

usual, is George Williams, perhaps the best canoe-man on the Fraser. He was on the Skeena River as early as 1906 and then transferred his activities to the Fraser, bringing scow loads of every conceivable kind of freight from the head of navigation at Tête Jaune Cache to the Fort George area, a distance of 315 miles.

The other two Indians in the inshore canoe are Jael, bow, and Amo, stern. The two white men are Arthur Holland, front, and Barnet, surveyors.

No man had a fuller and more adventurous life than George Williams. I knew him well from 1910 to 1916, and feel honoured in laying this belated tribute to his memory. The last trip I made on the Fraser was in George's cottonwood canoe, and always full of devilment, he couldn't resist the temptation of sending the canoe diving into the big swell at the head of the Cottonwood Canyon and giving his passengers a ducking.

George Williams was a man who readily gave credit where it was due. He frequently described his Fort George Native assistants as "the best of the best."

Many of the other scow pilots, as well as the people running rafts to the canyon, refused to believe there was any danger, and that the Canyon Cats were a bunch of thieves. They carried on, ignoring the warnings of others. Only when they found the canyon walls rising up around them, did they—in terror—fully realize the enormity of their errors.

There were exceptions, though, such as the two Scandinavian men that paddled a small raft into shore at South Fort George during the summer of 1912. A man named Bill Tuckwood happened to be standing on shore as they arrived, so they asked him how far it was to the Grand Canyon. These two men had already passed through it 166 kilometres upriver and hadn't realized it! We can only wonder what sort of monster they had been expecting.

Some greenhorns got through on luck alone, such as J.B. Manner. In 1913 he wrote this letter to the *Herald*:

. . . I left Wainwright [Alberta] about April 20. On arrival at Tête Jaune I found the water in the Fraser too low for navigation [for the steamers], so seven men and myself joined forces and built a scow. We made it to Fort George—315 miles in nine days. We came through safe, although we were all green hands at the business, but it was a trip I would not care to make in a scow again.

Mr. Manner was one of many that simply had no idea what they were up against. Somehow Lady Luck guided them safely through.

Several of the people who dared to face the downriver journey had strange tales to tell, such as Harry Sinclair, who ran away from his Chicago home at the age of twelve when his mother remarried after her husband's death. Harry made his way to Texas where, a few years later, he became a Texas Ranger. In due time Harry travelled to Montana and took up his chosen profession—gambling. One day the police raided his favourite establishment and a shootout occurred. Two of the men present were shot but Harry made his getaway, riding north to Edmonton. This was the start of his career as a café operator and, along with his newly acquired cook Eva, he followed the railway construction heading west. As was often the case, the café was only a front for the gambling that went on in the back room.

Soon Harry and Eva fell in love, got married and Eva became pregnant. This forced the couple to move on to something more permanent. Around June 1913, Harry left Eva in Tête Jaune, loaded their possessions in a scow and headed down the Fraser. Apparently his gambler's luck deserted him, because he lost most of their café equipment in the Grand Canyon.

When Harry arrived in South Fort George he opened a bathhouse, which once again was just a front for gambling. Two months later Eva joined him after a hazardous scow trip downriver. In fact she was so terrified that she never wanted to get into a boat again.

The story of the Sinclairs would be incomplete if I didn't add that during the winter of 1913–1914 they purchased a quarter-section of land at Chilako, west of Fort George, where they moved with their newborn son George. The move was undertaken during cold weather, which forced the family to improvise. Mother and son were bundled

Eva and Harry Sinclair in Edmonton, 1912. Courtesy E. Sinclair

inside a cardboard box that was covered with a blanket during the six-hour ride to their new home.

In due time much of the land was cleared and the family earned their living from Harry's gambling and a three-acre strawberry patch.

Many strange objects made their way down the mighty Fraser River during those years. The arrival by scow of a Heintzman piano in South Fort George was the talk of the town. Some of the people that arrived in boats or on rafts would pack their supplies around the Grand Canyon on foot and then let their crafts float through and hope for the best. Often only pieces were found at the bottom end. Some would gather up these pieces, patch them together and carry on, unaware that more rapids lay in wait farther down the river. The number of people arriving in South Fort George on rafts was considerable. The *Herald* stated that rafts were arriving every evening, and at times several were brought into shore at the same time.

Harry Sinclair beside his bathhouse in South Fort George, 1913. COURTESY E. SINCLAIR

Canyon 4 Tragedies

A stonished at the great loss of life along the upper Fraser River, the news media repeatedly called for more prevention work to be done. They called for signs to be placed above the canyons and rapids to warn of the dangers below and to show which channels to take. This, they stressed, would greatly reduce the loss of men and equipment.

Often the equipment that was lost was difficult to replace, such as the large donkey engine (a steam-driven tractor) that was being moved through the upper canyon when the scow capsized. For many years the tractor's smokestack could be seen protruding from its watery grave at low water levels.

During late summer 1911, the main railway contractors FW&S relocated their two big sternwheelers, *Operator* and *Conveyor*, which had finished their work on the Skeena River. They steamed to Vancouver where they were dismantled and shipped by way of Edmonton to the end of GTP steel. From that point the boilers, each weighing fifty thousand pounds (22,260 kg), were hauled—one with a donkey engine and the other with twelve teams of horses—to Tête

Jaune, another twenty miles along the grade. In one spot it took three days to move the boilers a distance of one mile.

Fir timbers were shipped from the coast for the reconstruction, and about two hundred men were employed in the rebuilding operation. The costs were staggering. These were huge boats, each with a gross weight of 700 tons, that were capable of carrying over 200 tons of freight as well as towing another 100 tons on scows, though their loads were limited to 150 tons because of the shallow water in the upper river. With ease they handled 90-ton steam shovels on barges, moving them along the waterway to wherever they were needed. These steamers took loaded scows or barges downriver to off-loading points or to the Grand Canyon, where they were handed over to scow pilots who moved them through the rapids to caches along the river or on to Fort George. Some pilots used powerboats to move several scows at one time, but the pilots without motors were forced to ride on the scows, with only the large sweeps or oars for control. Inexperienced pilots often paid the ultimate price when they were unable to control their scows and avoid the rocks. As well, there were many travellers on rafts or in small boats and canoes that had little or no concept of what lay in store for them when they faced the rapids and whirlpools of the Grand Canyon.

The whirlpool in the lower canyon showed its might to many throughout the years. It sometimes stood full-length cottonwood trees

Launching the steamer *Conveyor* at Tête Jaune, 1912. Courtesy Violet Baxter

on end and pulled them down out of sight. Often they would explode up out of the water some distance farther downriver. One newspaper article stated that soundings taken at this spot indicated over one-hundred-foot depths at high water levels.

A memorable story of the power of the whirlpool appeared in the *Herald* in 1912:

> Ludwig Wadman, a young German aged 26, was drowned yesterday in the Grand Canyon on the upper Fraser River. With two companions, Wadman had embarked at Tête Jaune Cache in a flat-bottomed boat, their goal being Fort George. Knowing nothing of the danger that awaited them, they paddled heedlessly downstream into the treacherous canyon whirlpool. Their frail craft was caught in the swirl and imme-diately capsized. The three men were thrown into the water, but the two survivors managed to cling to the boat and after being buffeted against the rocks, and whirling dizzily in the current, landed near the bank. Wadman was unable to reach the boat and was drawn under by the suction of the whirlpool. The survivors reached here today and informed the police of their companion's death.

The huge steamer *Operator* at Tête Jaune, 1912. Courtesy Prince George Public Library

Men who witnessed the boat's behaviour stated that the boat was not dragged under, as they usually were. Generally once the back of a boat reached the centre of the whirlpool the boat would stand on end and be pulled down. Apparently the difference in the action of the whirlpool was explained by whether it was filling or emptying at the time the craft went into it. Regardless, the other two men were indeed fortunate to survive.

As soon as the ice was off the river in 1912, an enterprising young man named Roy Spurr abandoned his café at Tête Jaune Cache because the action had moved a few miles to where FW&S had their huge cache. The reason the cache was built at this point was so it would be downstream of a mighty logjam that towered over ten metres high and blocked the entire river. When his business dried up Roy placed all his belongings on a scow and came down-river to the head of the Grand Canyon, where he built and operated a café and rooming house until the fall of 1913. This was a godsend to weary travellers or people who survived accidents in the canyon and needed assistance.

It was also during the summer of 1912 that FW&S built a huge warehouse above the upper canyon. Next they built a tramway from this warehouse to another reloading warehouse between the two canyons. After it was completed they moved many scows downriver with the big steamers *Conveyer* and *Operator*, where at the head of the canyon the material was off-loaded and hauled around the upper canyon with horses. It was then reloaded on scows and moved downriver by the independent scow operators. This prevented the enormous losses that had been occurring in the upper canyon, where FW&S had lost material equal to the value of two large sternwheelers. During their two years of operation, the warehouses, tramway and other expenses at the canyon cost FW&S the sum of $150,000. This is the equivalent of at least $7.5 million in today's currency.

The number of people drowned along the upper river during 1912 is unknown, but estimates suggest the number wasn't just high—it was astronomical. The media was correct when they screamed for more prevention in the way of signs placed along the river to point out the worst hazards. In his book *Bacon, Beans 'n Brave Hearts*, Russell

Walker states that the police had recovered eighty bodies from the Fraser River by the time it iced over for the winter. A few were found in the Hudson's Bay slough, or in other backeddies near Fort George.

The dangers presented along the river were not limited to summer, as countless horses were lost through the ice or due to other injuries. Often horses that died on the job were simply dumped into the river. Time was not wasted on such niceties as burying horses.

During the winter of 1912–1913, hundreds of teams of horses were hauling freight along the tote road from the end-of-steel to the Grand Canyon, where a massive amount of freight had accumulated for the 1913 scowing season.

Another winter project was undertaken at Fort George Canyon, where Captain Foster showed he was more than a steamer captain. With a crew of fourteen men he succeeded in removing several of the more dangerous rocks from the area around and above the canyon. At the same time another crew under W. McLaren was busy blasting boulders out of the river five miles below Fort George at Hudson's Bay Gardens (formerly Indian Gardens).

Regrettably, the blasting work came at least five years too late, as there were to be only two more full years of steamer service above Fort George.

By the time the river iced over in the fall of 1912, Frank Freeman and his crew of blasters had tamed the Giscome Rapids—with the aid of five hundred cases of dynamite—to the point that the rapids were no longer considered a threat to downriver traffic.

Another example of the problems faced by river travellers was shown in the following comments taken from the *Herald* on May 3, 1913:

> The ice from the upper river has not yet entirely gone out according to a report which reached here yesterday. Captain Bucey of the steamer *BC Express* left Quesnel some weeks ago for Tête Jaune Cache. Coming by way of Edmonton, he intended to look over the river on his way down by canoe, but is stalled up the river. Accompanied by A.K. Bouchier, he has had to walk some of the distance between here and the Cache on account of icejams. When last heard from

they were at Mile 195 [just west of Upper Fraser] waiting for Frank Freeman—the man who cleared the channel through Giscome rapids—to show them through and point out the new channel. Below Mile 185, near the Bear [Bowron] River, there was a large icejam yesterday and the two men had to wait for a channel to open in this jam before they could come through.

A point worth noting was that people canoeing the river in early spring or late fall were obliged to carry warm clothing and blankets in their canoes. The chance of getting caught in an icejam was ever-present, with the possibility of succumbing to exposure if they were unable to keep warm or make it to shore.

The *Herald* editorial again expressed its opinion of the river dangers in the May 31, 1913 edition:

> Scarcely a day has passed since the opening of navigation at the beginning of the present month, that reports have not reached here of the loss of life by drowning in the Fraser River between this point and Tête Jaune Cache. Between this place and the end of steel the distance by river is about 300 miles. The main line of the GTP follows the river in a general direction for this entire distance. There are three specific danger spots along this route in the northern Interior of BC from the present western end of the GTP. These are located upstream from this point as follows: the Goat River Rapids, about 200 miles; the Grand Canyon, about 106 miles, and Giscome Rapids, about 25 miles. Of these, the greatest danger is probably to be encountered in the Grand Canyon.
>
> Since the steel penetrated the Yellowhead Pass and gave access to the head of BC's greatest water lane, hordes of men bound upon all sorts of ventures into the much talked of "Fort George Country" have alighted from the GTP trains at Tête Jaune and have constructed for themselves craft of all descriptions on which they embark upon the broad bosom of the treacherous Fraser, bound downstream on their 300-mile journey.

Every arrival from the upper river tells of the thousands of scows, boats and canoes, which are either building, or are abroad upon the river, bound for this place. Every one of these craft must run the gauntlet of the rapids and canyons, and must successfully navigate the hundred and one danger spots between these places. In the known danger spots the average voyager will use every precaution against accident, and consequently the death toll from the canyons is not so large as would be expected from their forbidding character. The long rapids, however, and the hundreds of dangerous log-jams and riffles along the route, are daily claiming a record of deaths, which—considering the fact that the ice has only just left the river—is truly appalling.

The long list of accidents and deaths on this river leads us to voice a sentiment which we have long appreciated. Except to the big steamboats or power craft there is no safety in travel upon the waters of the upper Fraser River. The beginner on a three-piece raft may drift through the whole route along the river without harm, whilst the experienced bad-water canoe-men may meet with disaster, which all their knowledge of the river, and ability to handle a canoe, will not avail against.

. . . In spite of the lengthening list of "the dead" on the Fraser, and the fact that scores are drowned that are never even missed, the traffic from the steel head in crazy craft grows greater daily. The government of this province must realize their responsibility in this matter. If two powerful gasoline boats were placed on this river in charge of old rivermen, vested with the authority of provincial police, we believe that a great many of these drowning accidents could be averted. These boats could patrol the river and bring prisoners down from the camps, as well as warn and advise the raft and scow runners, and on occasions do rescue work.

Almost as if they had been listening, the June 2 edition of the *Edmonton Journal* noted:

SCOW BREAKS IN TWO,
FOUR MEN DROWN IN FRASER

Four men are reported to have been drowned last Friday in the Grand Canyon. This morning information was received in the city to the effect that four men, named St. John, Dutch, Dixon and William Kennedy, were drowned while going through the canyon on a scow. Rumour has it that the scow broke in two and the men were thrown into the water.

William Kennedy is the brother of Samuel Kennedy, the police constable at the King Edward Hotel. The latter stated this morning that he had received no word of the drowning, but said that his brother, William, had charge of a scow between Tête Jaune and Fort George. He went west last March after spending the winter at his former home in Alexandra, Ontario. Mr. Kennedy was employed on the scow all last summer, also.

The June 7 edition of the *Herald* noted:

Advices received just before going to press state that a scow was wrecked yesterday whilst running the Grand Canyon, and one man out of its six occupants was drowned. Some of the rescued men went four miles downstream on sweeps and bales of hay before they were rescued.

And in a backup to the story told from a different source, the same paper noted:

Within the next few days about 600 scow men will arrive here from the end of steel with a huge flotilla of laden scows. Some of these rivermen are quite without fear. The other day a scow broke up while running through the Grand Canyon. A scow man was rescued from where he clung to a log sweep. Four of his companions were drowned, but as soon as he got ashore he went to the head of the canyon and brought another scow through.

Early in 1913 a correspondent for the *Herald* was stationed at the canyon. On June 7 he reported, "A large barge representing some $10,000 [$500,000 in today's currency] containing a large boiler and 1000 feet of cable emerged from the gorge, turned turtle and deposited its load right below the big eddy. Another boiler was lost above the canyon."

The *Herald* editorial for June 14 read:

DEATH LURKS IN SEETHING VORTEX
OF GRAND CANYON

There have been no further reports of drowning accidents in the Grand Canyon this week, although several men have met their death between this place and that point. A provincial constable stationed at the canyon is refusing to allow men in small boats to run the canyon.

An old riverman has told the *Herald* that he has never seen the canyon in such a terrible state of disturbance as at present. The whirlpool in the lower canyon is now reaching out clear across the channel, where, in average stages of water, this terrible spot is local on the west side. This whirlpool can stand a huge tree straight up and draw it down deep into the vortex.

A riverman who watched the scows running the canyon one day last week stated to the *Herald* that the sight was awe inspiring. The huge lumbering craft, many of which are handled by men who know very little of river lore, come tearing down through the seething bedlam of the condensed channels, missing destruction by a few feet at every turn. That many of the men who are running the canyon do not realize the danger is obvious to rivermen.

Some of the scows are loaded with most valuable cargoes, and in one day last week over a quarter of a million dollars in value was run down through the Grand Canyon in scows. One scow alone, loaded with tobacco, carried a cargo worth $25,000.

The same day—June 14—the reporter at the canyon wrote:

The canyon has commenced to take its toll of human lives. The recent fatal accident, in which four lives were lost, has weeded out the amateurs from amongst the scow-men. Now not so many of the men treat the passage of the upper rapids as a joke or as a bluff perpetrated by a few of the river-men with the designed end of creating a monopoly at expensive rates of canyon pilots. There is no doubt that a lot of the scows that went through at first were lucky—durned lucky—but now that the water has risen so high it is management and a knowledge of the new conditions and the new channel caused by the blowing up of the rocks during the winter that is more and more the factor of safety and that bull-headed nerve is without special knowledge and very liable to be fatal.

. . . A portion of the scow that was broken and caused the accident was recovered and is now lying tied to the bank above Camp 182. It looks as if the scow had been broken across just as if some giant had snapped a toy box across his knee. The cargo must have all been spilt into the water. No sign of the bodies has been discovered and from current report it is unlikely that they will be. The rapids do not give up their dead.

The Tonequah River has been in flood all the past week and the scows and freight boats carrying supplies to camps 176, 177 and 172 report deep water all the way up.

This last paragraph surprised me no end—the fact that freight boats and scows were taken up what is now Moxley Creek, a narrow stream that can be difficult to traverse even in a small boat. Further, it shows that they serviced the camp at Mile 172, which is near Boulder Creek, just short of Toneko Lake (formerly Tonequah Lake.) It seems fair to suggest that these rivermen were in a class by themselves where navigation was concerned.

Their knowledge of river lore wasn't common to all, as this report before the middle of June clearly shows: ". . . Since the beginning of the season over twenty men have been drowned in the Grand Canyon."

And yet again: "During one week in early June [1913] four rafts were lost in the Canyon."

Just a few days later, on June 21, this article appeared:

> Since last week there have been several additional accidents at the canyon; the lower canyon taking a hand in the fatal game. The whirlpool in the lowest canyon has assumed formidable dimensions and commenced to prove an additional menace to the freight boats on the river. A small Peterboro [canoe] last Sunday was lined down the upper canyon and the two men who made up the crew were warned and advised to line down the lower reach. But laughing all such advice to scorn they boldly rushed out into the spray of the first rapid, which they shot safely. Then they rushed out into the whirlpool, where despite all their frenzied efforts, they stayed almost stationary till the stern of the canoe worked into the centre of the vortex, when suddenly the stern was sucked below the surface. The canoe stood straight on end and dived underneath, stern first, with its human occupants. The man at the bow, by a lucky fluke, managed to escape, being dragged down and struggled ashore, but his companion did not reappear.

In fairness to FW&S, the main contractors, it must be noted that they had a boat stationed in the lake between the two canyons. If a vessel capsized or a scow came apart in the upper canyon, this boat was signaled by a watchman standing high on the rock cliff. If any survivors reached the lake, the men in the boat rescued them.

Another *Herald* article stated:

> One of the Canyon Cats, A.H. Dieber, better known as "Sandbar Slim," had a narrow escape while running the upper canyon. One of the sweeps broke and his scow hit Green's Rock with such force that the entire deck was torn off and deposited right into the worst part of the current with him

on it. Only by the greatest luck did the two pieces come back together and "Slim" manage to make it to safety.

One day a fully loaded scow emerged from the canyon with no one aboard. A short distance downriver, two homesteaders saw it drifting by so they rowed out in their dugout canoes and towed the derelict ashore. While they were busy unloading a wealth of goods, a second scow appeared with the original scow-men aboard. It seems one of the sweeps had broken right in the heart of the canyon, so the pilots had scrambled aboard the other scow in an effort to save themselves. The homesteaders gave up their prize reluctantly, feeling that finders should be keepers.

During the early summer of 1913 the provincial constable stationed at the head of the canyon earned his keep. He refused to allow small boats to enter the canyon, making them either portage around or line their boats through. He also greatly assisted the Canyon Cats when he demanded that all scows must have four experienced oarsmen at the sweeps before they were allowed to enter the canyon. As well, scow-loads were restricted to a maximum of fifteen-tons. Even with all these safety precautions, there was still a great loss of life and material. The main reason for the greater number of deaths in 1913 was the increased traffic flow on the river.

Elmer Micks of Terrace, BC, gave me an example of what these first-time voyageurs faced in the upper river. He sent me a taped interview made in 1974 with his aunt, Doris Ferland. Quizzed by her grandson John Ferland, Doris relived her family's trip from Nebraska to Marten Lake, seven miles east of Fort Fraser. The year was 1913 when Doris, at age thirteen, accompanied her parents Ermine and Graham Micks on this memorable journey. The family had sold their 360-acre farm in Nebraska; the money from the sale was desperately needed on their long journey.

The portion of their trip that drew my attention was Graham's hazardous journey down the Fraser River. Please take note that Doris, at age seventy-four, is recalling memories that took place when she was thirteen years of age. Following are some excerpts from that interview:

DORIS: . . . We went to Calgary first, and then we went to Edmonton because we were going to British Columbia and Dad bought up some milk cows and horses and chickens and two brand-new ranges [stoves] and all kinds of cupboards and chairs and beds and couches and stuff. He bought that after we got to Edmonton and then he rented a boxcar and loaded it up with all the stuff. We also had pure retriever dogs, black ones, which were just puppies at the time. Anyway, we took all that stuff to Tête Jaune Cache, which was the leading end of the railroad at that time.

JOHN: Was that in British Columbia?

DORIS: Yes. They were just building the railroad at that time so we had to go by boat toward Prince George [Fort George]. I think it was the B.X. [The women and children rode on the sternwheeler *BC Express,* while the men travelled by scow.] My father bought a scow and paid seven hundred dollars for it, and the Austin brothers also bought a scow. Mutt and Jeff we called them—our scow was Jeff and theirs was Mutt, and it turned out to be a mutt too. They [the Austins] were taking real good horses to Prince George to sell, and we got to this big eddy [Grand Canyon] where they wouldn't let the passengers ride through; you had to get off and walk around this eddy. Well, when they went to take the scow through this eddy, they wouldn't let them start unless they had two scow-men [Canyon Cats] to accompany them. So my dad and Henry and the two scow-men went to go through and they were told that they had to get two more scow-men or they would not be allowed to go on. And of course sometimes they missed. Anyway, when the Austin brothers went through with their scow Mutt, they didn't hit it at the right time so their scow went down. Their horses were pawing at the bank trying to get out of the river and my dad said, "Well if that's what can happen . . . " They wanted Dad to unload all the horses and cows and the piano but Dad said, "What is the use of me unloading all this stuff—the horses and the cattle, the chickens and the furniture and everything, because if the scow goes down, they might just as well go with it." So they hired two more guides and went through and they hit it just right. You see, if you hit it [the whirlpool] when it was emptying it would shoot you right out, but if you hit it when it was filling it would suck you down.

Doris and her mother rode on the sternwheeler *BC Express* while the men took the scows through the canyons. Doris went on to describe how all the passengers had to walk around the upper canyon, while the captain and crew took the steamer on through and picked them up below. When Doris and her mother arrived in Fort George they spent several anxious days waiting until Graham safely arrived with the loaded scow.

Obviously the Micks were forced to hire the Canyon Cats by the policeman stationed at the top of the upper canyon, and there is no doubt that this policeman faced a thankless task in trying to protect people from their own ignorance regarding the forces and dangers of the canyon. In one instance the policeman informed the media that the body of a man named George Seacord was pulled from the river three miles below the canyon. He confirmed that this body was the only one recovered of the last twelve men drowned.

Coinciding with the arrival of the policeman was the placement of a large sign above the canyon, warning of the dangers below and indicating the safe channel to be followed. The *Herald* of June 21, 1913, noted:

Action is now taken by the government in the manner of the protection of life on the Fraser River as far as is practicable, through government agent Herne here, who acted in conjunction with the forest department, whose rangers did the work. Large signs have been painted and posted on the river above many dangerous riffles and logjams warning the small craft of the dangers below them and directing them into the right channels. These signs are four feet by eight feet.

In retrospect it seems regrettable that all of the media attention did not manage to have the signs posted four years earlier, as so many lives would have been saved and much less equipment lost. Once a scow with five thousand feet of cable lost its load in the upper canyon. Fortunately all the crew managed to make shore.

That a huge quantity of freight was being moved downriver at that time was made apparent by an article in the *Herald* dated August 2, 1913. It told how George Williams and two other pilots named Bob Alexander and William McLaren had moved over sixty scows downriver since the opening of navigation in May. It further stated that this constituted over one thousand tons of freight.

A story with a rather odd twist unfolded in 1913 when two Frenchmen, Maurice Streiff and Samuel Tonduz, lost their scow and were reported drowned in the canyon. Several days later the Belgian Consulate in Edmonton, which looked after French affairs in the area, sent a man named Maurice Poldt to investigate. He arrived in Fort George on the steamer *BC Express*, hoping to find the bodies and claim them for burial. As he toured the bunkhouses and lunch counters seeking information, he suddenly walked right into Mr. Tonduz, who informed him that he and his companion had indeed lost their scow but both had managed to make it to shore. Mr. Streiff had abandoned his plan of becoming a river pilot and had walked back to Tête Jaune. As for Mr. Tonduz, after escaping the river he had gone to work on the adjacent railway grade. One day he was watching a blast when a flying rock pierced the heart of an Italian standing right beside him. At that point Mr. Tonduz quickly decided that this was not his line of work either and walked the fifty miles to Fort George.

A regular visitor to the canyon in 1913 was the steamer *BC Express*, which had the Royal Mail contract. It was the first sternwheeler to carry a load of freight and passengers to Tête Jaune, and the only one to offer a scheduled service between there and Fort George.

This gallant vessel made many memorable trips. Mr. Willis West, manager of the BC Express Company, detailed one example. In an article published in the *BC Historical Quarterly*, July–October 1949 issue, Mr. West described his trip to the Grand Canyon in June 1913:

> When we arrived at the canyon, I accompanied Capt. Bucey on his hike to inspect the whirlpool. The trail along the high rock wall of the canyon was rough, and in places it was necessary to climb ladders made of poles to get to the higher levels

of the trail. A point on the high ramparts of rock was soon reached from where the whirlpool could be viewed directly below. It was an awesome sight to watch the full volume of water in the Fraser pour through a narrow gap from the basin into the raging maelstrom, which seemed to be created by the peculiar rock formation of the riverbed. The whirlpool extended about 200 feet from shore to shore and was continually emptying and filling. There did not seem to be a great deal of driftwood coming down from the basin, and Capt. Bucey, after studying the scene for a while, decided it would be safe to proceed.

After making sure that the passengers were all aboard, the captain turned his ship into the stream. Soon the whirlpool was reached and with a full head of steam the BC Express was steered into it. When the steamer had reached the strong current running into the narrow channel leading up into the basin, she appeared to hesitate, and then started to drift back into the whirlpool. Although Capt. Bucey tried several times to steam up through the gap, the ship was unable to make progress against the strong current. The captain then decided it would be necessary to line her through, and he started, therefore, to maneuver his ship over to the left side of the

The BC Express in the Grand Canyon, 1913. BC ARCHIVES A-07835

canyon. Suddenly a spruce tree about seventy feet in length with a large root appeared on the surface of the whirlpool, and before the steamer could avoid it, it had swept underneath her and lodged against her three main rudders. Held there by the strong current, the spruce tree put the steering gear out of commission and the captain lost control of his ship. The tree was so lodged against the ship's rudders that when she went ahead, she turned sharply towards the left of the canyon, and when she steamed astern her stern would likewise swing to the left. Fortunately, the stern-wheel was not obstructed nor damaged in any way, so the captain began to maneuver the ship by means of the wheel. His plan was to drop the ship downstream to a point where the canyon wall was low enough to put a deck hand ashore with a line. Then the ship could be tied up, and the ship's carpenter and deck crew put to the work detaching the rudders in order to dislodge the spruce from under the ship.

. . . The captain would signal to the engine-room for slow speed ahead, then, when the nose of the ship would reach the wall of the canyon, he would signal for the engines to be stopped so that the ship could drift downstream with the current. She was still in the whirlpool and had just touched the canyon wall with her bow when suddenly a heavy-set male passenger raced across the forward deck and leaped onto a narrow ledge of the rock. He had barely landed on the ledge when the steamer drifted away and he was left clinging to the rock barely six feet above the surface of the turbulent whirlpool.

Finally the steamer whirled about and drifted away. About half an hour later the captain got a line ashore and, after securing the ship, sent a party to attempt the rescue of the frightened passenger. As the party reached the spot and looked down over the cliff they were surprised to find him still clinging there seventy feet below them. A small man was lowered with a rope and they were both hauled up the canyon wall and rescued.

The following day the steamer retraced its journey up the lower canyon, where, because the whirlpool was emptying instead of filling, it went through without a problem.

Mr. West went on to describe the courage of the Canyon Cats:

> Just the previous week five men had been thrown into the rushing current when their scow had struck a rock, and only the leader [Joe McNeil] of the crew had been rescued by the lifeboat [stationed in the bay between the canyons]. The other four were never seen again, but the rescued leader had immediately walked to the upper end of the canyon and without a trace of reluctance had brought another scow downstream and was still imperturbably working as a pilot.

The *Herald* editor expressed his view of the Canyon Cats by writing:

> Canyon Cats is the name given in the GTP construction camps for the daredevils along the upper Fraser who pilot scows laden with railway supplies through the canyon. To be a Cat one must have nerve, plus. No self-respecting casualty company would insure their lives for a penny. Daily they stare into the bright eyes of danger. Time and again until the tale becomes monotonous from the telling, the scows have been broken to bits in the rapids and their freight and the men who piloted them cover the bottom of the river. Water is now low in the Fraser and workmen are salvaging the freight lost earlier in the season. Meanwhile, running the canyon goes on, but with the advance of the GTP construction, a safe way will soon replace the dangerous river. The "Canyon Cats" who are lucky enough to outguess the swift-running Fraser will have big stakes to their credit, for they will collect over $1000 each for every month of the season.

From the construction camps a correspondent wrote on June 17, 1913:

> Writing from Camp 180 [present day Sinclair Mills], the show camp on the river, and also the first post below the canyon,

the waterway presents quite a busy scene. During the past two days the steamer *Chilcotin* has been up and down again from the canyon. The steamer *BC Express* went up a couple of days ago en route to Mile 53, and has safely passed the dangerous rapids of the upper canyon.

On an average eight or nine scows have passed daily down the Fort George direction. Yesterday two scow-loads of horses, others containing dump cars, rails and equipment. Here and there private scows containing spuds and fresh vegetables with which their owners intend to make a big strike en route and at Fort George, their terminus. Spuds at seven cents this far down is a fair measure of their variety.

I hear that the waters of the canyon have begun to take their toll this early in the season. Last year and previously the toll exacted has been in human lives, but it was hoped that now that the rocks and shelves had been blown out and the channels somewhat cleared of obstructions so that safety in a large measure could be assured. I am told by the scow-men that the water through the rapids is much faster this year than before; that the removal of the rocks has not only created a quicker current but that the increased volume sets direct upon the big rock at the base of the second rapid and that a new channel of safety must be followed or disaster ensues.

This last week three scows have become a total wreck, one belonging to a Fort George firm, spreading its load of supplies far and away down the river. Boatmen and rafters were very busy during the passage of the goods and some good salvaging is reported below here.

. . . I was impressed by a boatload of Ontario fruit-growers who came down in a boat the other day en route to Fort George or further down the river. They were enthusiastic over the soil and considered that the cultivation of that fruit alone on the river banks would be a large item in the growth and the prosperity of the upper Fraser.

Everyone that one sees along the grade and on the river, and there are some hundreds in the week, are all making for Fort George.

By mid-summer 1913 the policeman stationed at the canyon took matters in hand and created much bad will because of it. He forced very strict rules on those coming downriver. Scows were forced to have eight Canyon Cats on them before they entered the canyon. All scows with a load over fifteen tons had to unload and portage their supplies around the upper canyon. As well, all small craft had to be lined down through the upper rapids. As irritating as his regulations must have seemed, had this action been taken four years earlier a great number of lives and much value in supplies would have been saved.

Just to give an idea how much traffic was going through the canyon during 1913 I quote an article in the *Herald* dated August 19, 1913:

MANY SCOWS GO THROUGH THE CANYON

There is some talk of building a road from Roy Spurr's canyon stopping place at the immediate head of the upper canyon to the road now connecting the upper and lower warehouses, for portage purposes. This would cut off a good half the haul round the upper canyon and at the rate the water is falling, portaging will soon become necessary for a good portion of the cargo on the heavily loaded boats.

Canyon pilots are taking an average of 15 scows through the canyon per day. Last Wednesday the FW&S pilots took 15 scows through the canyon between 7 a.m. and 2 p.m. with an hour taken for dinner. This is the best record for quick work to date.

When we consider the steamers that were plying the canyon area from both directions and then add in the scows, rafts, canoes and boats of all sizes and shapes, including motorized launches, it becomes readily apparent that the canyon was a buzz of activity during the summer of 1913.

One of the boats that was plying the waterway was described in the *Herald* in this manner:

The *St. George*, the newest motorboat for express, passenger and freight service between Tête Jaune Cache and Fort George on the Fraser River, will be placed in commission on Tuesday next. It has been built entirely in Edmonton, and is fitted up with every convenience to be found in a motorboat. It is of 40-hp and will be capable of accommodating some 24 passengers and hauling approximately ten tons of freight . . . An experienced man has been engaged to pilot the *St. George*, which will make the return trip in five days.

Regrettably, no evidence could be found to confirm that this boat made the round trip in five days. If it did, it was a considerable achievement. Moving twenty-four passengers and up to ten tons of supplies a distance of 630 miles (1,014 km) through canyons and rapids in five days—with a 40-horsepower engine—appears to defy logic.

The courage of these pioneers was undeniable and even the steamer captains showed off at times. Several of them pitted their vessels against the wild waters of the upper canyon, but the big steamer *Conveyor* under Captain Shannon was the only one to climb through without a line. On four different occasions it climbed the upper rapids in fifteen minutes under its own power. When the steamer *Hammond* tried, it found itself at a standstill right in the fastest water and only by getting a line to shore was disaster averted.

The steamer *BC Express* was by far the most versatile on the upper river, and time and again she proved it. During June 1913 she set the record for the 315-mile run from Tête Jaune to Fort George, completing it in forty-two hours with a full load of freight and eighty passengers. As for its captain, the *Herald* noted:

Captain Bucey is performing a great service for this country, and he is performing this service well. Already [in June] he has successfully navigated the steamer *BC Express* on four round trips to Tête Jaune Cache since the opening of navigation, covering a distance of over 2,500 miles.

But the captain has a long record of success as a river navigator. He worked on the command of the Hudson's Bay Company's steamboats in northern waters, that are navigable to the sea, for over 12 years. Along the Skeena River he bears the reputation of being a great riverman, and a record of having run the Kitselas Canyon at the highest stage of water.

On every trip the captain makes to Tête Jaune he faces the Grand Canyon, with its seething whirlpool and death record. With a $75,000 [$3.75 million in today's currency] steamboat obeying the turn of his hand, the captain runs the canyon where other boats line their way down, and he runs it with his white flyer with knowledge of his ability to run it successfully.

Captain Bucey is an old Mississippi captain. He never strays very far from his boat, and has little to say for himself even when pressed for information about his work. He is a typical sailor man, one of those we would expect to see on the flying bridge of an ocean liner.

The praise extended to Captain Bucey was certainly justified. Those of us who have travelled this waterway realize just how difficult it is to successfully navigate the upper river with a small riverboat in low water. In my view, all steamer captains earned the respect awarded them.

Several other steamers made regular trips to the canyon in 1913, hauling passengers and supplies downriver from the canyon—among them the B.X. and the *Chilcotin*, but the days of the steamers on the upper river were numbered. When word reached the *Herald* that low-level bridges were being placed across the river, which would stop steamer traffic, the following editorial appeared:

At Dome Creek, 156 miles up the Fraser from this point, the first bridge crossing is now ready for the barricading of the river. The cement abutments are in place and the steel is on the ground. Material for this bridge has been delivered some distance ahead of the steel, and even if steel were laid to that point it would be some time before general freight would be delivered at a point where it could be reached by steamboats below the bridge. There is another bridge where the same thing applies about 85 miles above here [Hansard Bridge].

This matter should be dealt with immediately. The railroad company must not for a moment be allowed to tie up the delivery of freight in this section ahead of their steel. They can find means for the delivery of their own freight over the steel that is in the contractors' hands, but not for the use of the public, the consideration of whom must be gained through their own efforts.

The type of bridges to be used on this river, we understand, are without swing or draw spans, and when completed, will shut off the navigation of the river effectually for steamboats owing to their low levels. We are not worrying about this, as the steel looks good to the *Herald*, but there are those who regret to see the river blocked. There is no doubt that a fine tourist route will thus be obliterated if the plans of the railroad concern are carried into effect.

The rumours were true, and by the end of August 1913 the low-level bridge at Mile 146 (Dome Creek) blocked the river to the big steamers. Captain Bucey was on his unlucky thirteenth trip of the season to Tête Jaune Cache when he encountered a cable across the river. Coaxed by others, he restrained his first impulse, which was to take a shotgun ashore to settle the matter.

Acting out of self-defence, the railroad had to eliminate the competing steamers, which were delivering freight at half the price the railroad would have had to charge to stay in business. Since the railroad—which was a year-round enterprise necessary to the developing Interior—had to succeed, the illegal bridges were allowed to stand. The BC Express Company fought the illegal blockage in court, first in Vancouver, where they won, and then in the Supreme Court, where they lost by a three-to-two decision. Finally in 1918 the BC Express Company applied to the Judicial Committee of the Privy Council in London for leave to appeal. When the hearing took place a junior counsel was appointed to represent the Express Company. He was no match for the opposition's brilliant counsel Leighton McCathy, and so the Express Company had to swallow a final loss as well as court costs. Their damage claim for $75,000 was thrown out.

Denied river access, the freight and passenger traffic disappeared except for small riverboats, and the famous canyon lost favour with the media.

The BC Express Company was not the only business hurt by the closure of the river. All along the upper river, homesteaders had taken up land in the belief that they had river transportation available to them. Many people who had previously been served by the steamers were suddenly cut off because they were on the opposite side of the Fraser River from the rail service. Many stopping places, including Roy Spurr's establishment at the head of the canyon, were forced to close. All along the upper stretch of the river, old homesteads can still be seen from an aircraft. What is not generally known, though, is that all the original homesteaders between the Big Salmon (McGregor) River and Tête Jaune—a distance of 212 miles (340 km)—were squatters. There was a reserve along that stretch of the river that extended for three miles across the valley floor. This reserve had been put in place to protect the railroad from having to acquire property at expensive rates from homesteaders who would have claimed land along the right-of-way ahead of the railway surveyors. When the reserve was lifted in June 1914 many of these squatters were eventually rewarded by obtaining title to their land. Others simply gave up and moved away, or moved closer to the small communities that were springing up around sawmills, which eventually became the main source of employment throughout the area.

The 5teamers

The arrival of the steamers, also called sternwheelers and paddle-wheelers, heralded the dawn of a new age in central BC. Prior to their arrival, pack trains comprised of horses and dog teams delivered most of the goods to distant places. This was a difficult and tedious system that often meant months of painfully slow travel through the forests. At times they were delayed by flooded streams. Strong winds that blew trees across their trails, as well as early snowstorms, made deliveries arrive late and thereby increased the cost.

The resolve required to move goods and supplies before the arriv-al of the steamers is well demonstrated in the following article taken from the *Herald* dated September 17, 1910:

INLAND WATERWAYS

That the advantages of the inland waterways of the North are becoming recognized more every day is a significant fact. Freight which for years past has gone in by way of Essington; thence to Hazelton by steamer; Babine Lake by packhorse; thence by schooner to Stewart's Lake [Stuart Lake]; down Stewart's Lake to Fort St. James and by packhorse to MacLeod Lake [McLeod Lake]. Then the freight for Fort Graham is loaded into scows again for the 160-mile trip. It is understood that the following route is being used for the first time this year—from Victoria to South Fort George; thence to Giscombe Portage by the Fort George Lumber and Navigation Company's plucky little boat *Chilco*; thence over the height of land to Summit Lake and on down Crooked River to MacLeod Lake. This effects a saving of four cents a pound over the old Hazelton route, and also a great deal of time . . .

The saving mentioned above may not seem like much, but it is comparable to $1.60 a pound in today's currency. Put another way, it would add the equivalent of $160 to a hundred-pound sack of flour.

The steamers played an integral part in the development of the interior of BC, and for that reason a brief description of the twelve steamers that worked the upper Fraser River is in order.

First I want to point out that some of the early-day steamers were called sidewheelers, because they had a drive wheel on each side. This was a poor system in that these steamers were unable to approach the shore of a stream or lake without the danger of damaging the drive wheels. When the sternwheelers came into use their superiority was immediately evident, as they could approach shore almost anywhere and still have their drive wheel out in deep water.

Most sternwheelers discharged their steam directly into the smokestack, creating a draft similar to a forge. For this reason these vessels were able to burn damp to wet wood picked directly off the bars along the rivers.

Referring to the total of three hundred steamers that worked BC and Yukon rivers, Art Downs wrote in his magnificent book *Sternwheel Days:*

> Despite being ripped open in rapids, gutted by fires, swamped in storms, crushed by ice and torn apart by boiler explosions, they served where needed and for as long as required—100 years.

The first real hint of change on the upper Fraser River occurred in 1871 when the little steamer *Enterprise*, built in 1863, came through Fort George and made its way up the Nechako River in an attempt to service the Omineca goldfields. Though it failed in that objective, this gallant vessel made its way through Stuart, Trembleur and Takla Lakes. It was eventually abandoned on Trembleur Lake, which at that time was known as Tremblay Lake.

Another steamer that worked the Quesnel–Soda Creek run was the *Victoria*. It was launched at Quesnel in 1868 and worked along the run until 1886, when it was abandoned near Fort Alexandria.

After the visit of the *Enterprise*, the Fort George area returned to its normal state of isolation for another thirty-seven years. When the steamer *Charlotte*, launched in Quesnel in 1896, blew its whistle at South Fort George in 1908, it truly heralded the dawn of a new age, for it introduced passenger and freight traffic to the area for the first time. It didn't take long for the 111-x-20-foot *Charlotte* to prove that it was a hazardous occupation moving steamers through the Fort George Canyon and other rapids along the river.

For example, after thirteen years of service without an accident, the *Charlotte* started a run of bad luck when its winching cable slipped off a steel pin on the wall of Fort George Canyon twenty-four kilometres downriver from Fort George. The *Herald* of May 21, 1910, noted:

> The steamer *Charlotte* met with an accident Friday morning while Captain Alexander was lining his vessel through Fort George Canyon, and is now lying at the foot of the Canyon safe, but with some three feet of water in her hold. Captain Alexander came down in the steamer's skiff last evening bringing word of the unfortunate, but not wholly serious accident, to his managers and owners, the James Reid Estate. The accident occurred at 8 o'clock in the morning, and was caused by the cable slipping off the pin on the shore as the steamer was giving way to the current. When the steamer lost its hold on shore the current swung the bow around and the captain was unable to control her any longer. She struck on

a rock and stove a hole in her side allowing the water to pour in. With considerable skill Captain Alexander beached his boat at the foot of the canyon and after sending two men to Fort George to notify Captain Bonser of the steamer *Chilco* to come and get his passengers, hurried to Quesnel to arrange for shipping wrecking material by the steamer *Quesnel* to repair the craft.

As customary all the passengers were walking over the portage at the time the accident occurred and no one was injured, and the cargo is not damaged. The *Charlotte* was heavily loaded this trip, a great part of the cargo being a shipment of lumber from Harry Joyce's mill.

After that accident and another similar near-catastrophe in Cottonwood Canyon, all pins were required by law to have an eye or a ring on the end of the pin so the cable could not slip off and leave the steamers to the mercy of the canyons. It is interesting to note that the steamer captains ignored this rule.

Steamer *Enterprise* at Soda Creek. This plucky vessel travelled the waterways to Takla Lake in 1871. BC Archives A-03908

Repaired and back in service, just a month went by before the *Charlotte* had another accident in Fort George Canyon. The *Herald* wrote:

The accident occurred at the head of the canyon. The wind and current were too strong at a dangerous point and it was impossible to control the course of the steamer. She was forced at full speed bow first onto a rock, causing a collision of such force as to stave in the stem post. The jar caused a shifting forward of the boiler several inches, breaking the steam connections and enveloping the vessel and passengers in a cloud of steam. A panic ensued among the twenty-some passengers, and in a moment's time most everyone had a life preserver on. The chief engineer, Parrie, stuck to his post, however, and answered every bell of Captain Alexander, and the steamer was brought safely to mooring on the east bank. The firemen raked the fires out and saved the vessel from further difficulty. In a few hours the boiler was shifted back into place, the steam pipes again connected and the voyage continued to Quesnel.

The steamer *Charlotte* at Quesnel. BC Archives B-01206

Perhaps it is true that bad luck strikes in threes. At least that was the case with the *Charlotte*, because a month later the old vessel was involved in another wreck. On July 23, the *Herald* noted:

> The last and third accident the *Charlotte* has had this season occurred on her voyage down the river last Friday from Fort George. Captain Foster had taken his vessel practically through the canyon [Fort George] when it was noticed that she was beginning to fill. It is stated by those on board that there had been no perceptible jar by striking the rocks, though the water being high, the vessel was thrown about considerably by the current. It is presumed, however, that she must have struck a sunken reef at the point just above the last gorge, which at very low water is sometimes showing. The other conjecture is that the weakening caused to the hull by the two former accidents and the pitching of the craft through the canyon combined to so strain the hull as to open the seams and permit her to fill very rapidly.
>
> When Captain Foster saw how rapidly the boat was filling with water, the only thing to do was to beach the boat, and with consummate skill he was able to direct the course of the waterlogged and half-filled craft to the lower end of the first bar below the mouth of the canyon. The boat was heavily listed to starboard and it appeared to those on board that she was going to "turn turtle." No doubt this would have happened had the captain not been able to throw his crippled craft against the sandbar, thus righting her.

Though there was just one lifeboat on the *Charlotte*, all the passengers got safely to shore and heaped great credit on the captain and crew for their bravery and attention to duty. First Engineer Parrie stayed at his post until the water was up to his neck. The captain stayed at the wheel until the rising water forced him to climb out the window of the pilothouse.

A touch of panic gripped the ship's passengers when the ship first started sinking. One of the passengers jumped overboard and with great difficulty managed to swim to shore.

After basic repairs were made, an attempt was made to steam back to Quesnel. At one point it was necessary to tear out all the partitions on the lower deck just to get enough fuel to keep the pumps and the main engine going. After a complete inspection in Quesnel the proud old steamer yielded to the "three strikes you're out" rule and went into a deserved retirement. Worth noting is that while Captain Alexander piloted the vessel during the first two accidents, Captain Foster was at the wheel for the third. This leaves one to wonder if Captain Alexander was relieved of his duties in the interim.

When the steamer *Nechacco*, launched at Quesnel in 1909, arrived at Fort George in 1909, history was about to be made. This eighty-by-sixteen-foot steamer was designed for shallow water, with a draught of only thirteen inches, and it proved its worth by fighting its way up the Nechako River to Noonla (Fraser Lake) during the month of June. For an encore, it moved on to greater achievements by steaming up the Fraser River to tackle the mighty Grand Canyon, which until that time had been considered impassable to steamers. Captain Bonser had three rings placed on the canyon walls and by the use of a capstan (winch), lined his vessel through the canyon. He then continued on upriver to the head of the Goat River Rapids, 324 kilometres upstream of Fort George, which was a magnificent achievement. Though some history books state that he made the trip right to Tête Jaune, newspapers of the time claim that he was forced to drop his load of supplies near the head of the Goat River Rapids because of low water levels in the river.

The *Nechacco's* well-earned glory was short lived, because in November 1909 she was stopped by ice at Fort George Canyon, where all the supplies were taken ashore. The story of what happened next was carried in the *Fort George Tribune* on November 27, 1909:

> The crew of the *Nechacco* is still here. The plan arranged for leaving a week ago miscarried. The men were to break trail from the steamboat 12 to 14 miles to a connection with the Blackwater road, where they would be met by a sleigh from Fort George. Instead of breaking trail to the Blackwater road, they broke trails to Fort George, where they arrived in ones, twos and threes, more or less exhausted. N.S. Clarke headed a

search party that was out all one night and managed to bring in the engineer and purser. The last brought in was a cook, a Japanese-Chinese boy called "Billy." He had work to do that prevented him from leaving with the others.

Billy was instructed how to follow the others but was not clothed for cold weather or for breaking a trail. When found, he had been out three days without food and both his feet were frozen. He was brought to Fort George and preparations were made to bring a doctor from Barkerville, 240 kilometres distant. But the next morning the boy's feet did not look bad and the danger of losing them had passed.

As for all the off-loaded freight, a man named Jim Dunn spent two weeks cutting a trail to the canyon from the Blackwater Road, then hauled the supplies to South Fort George.

The steamer *Nechacco* fought several battles with the rapids along the Nechako (meaning "big fish river" because of its sturgeon populations). The White Mud, Upper White Mud (Sestino) and Isle de Pierre (Stone) Rapids were the worst, but the rapids near the mouth of the Stuart River (Chinlac) also posed problems in low water levels. A rugged little ship, the *Nechacco* was damaged several times, with the result that during the winter of 1909–1910 it was rebuilt and renamed *Chilco*. The next summer it was again damaged when it attempted to run the Chinchula Rapids eighty kilometres south of Fort George. Not in the least daunted by these accidents, the captain got another scare while lining up the Isle de Pierre Rapids on the Nechako River. They had made their way about halfway up the rapids when the tree they were lined to pulled out of the ground and sent the ship back into the rapids, totally out of control. Water gained entry into the lower deck and then into the firebox, adding the potential for an explosion. Worse yet, this meant there was no power to regain control. Only by the greatest bit of luck did the vessel stop against a sandbar, and within a few hours repairs were completed.

As it turned out, the *Chilco* used up all of its allotted luck when it got into an accident at Chinlac in October. After it survived that ordeal, it was bringing a load of freight up from Quesnel when it found the Fort George Canyon blocked with ice. The ship was beached seven miles upstream from the Blackwater River, where the freight was unloaded and taken ashore. A short time later ice jammed at the mouth of the river. This caused the water to rise about twelve feet (almost 4 m), breaking the *Chilco* free of its moorings. When last seen that fall only the pilothouse protruded above the water. The following April the crew managed to refloat the vessel and attempted to run to Quesnel for repairs. When they checked out Cottonwood Canyon, they found it jammed with ice. What happened next was reported in the *Herald* of May 13, 1911:

> The causes leading up to the loss of the *Chilco* last month, as reported to the inspector of boilers at Vancouver, show that the accident was due to the bursting of the boiler above the canyon while running for safety upriver to avoid the jam. Captain Ritchie says, "We left our winter quarters at 11:30 and landed at La Voice's at 1:30, where we took on three cords of wood. Left at 2:00 and went to Pedley and Smith's, where we took on wood and tied up for supper. Left there at 5:30 and went down to Cottonwood Canyon. Saw it was impossible to get through. Walked down to the canyon. Started back upriver, running for safety to clear the ice. The boiler blew up two and a half miles above the canyon. Nobody knew exactly what the trouble was. Could not get a line to shore. The boat then drifted into the canyon and at 6:30 landed gently against the ice. At 11:00 that night she broke up. The following morning between 5:00 and 6:00 I saw her hull, which looked as if it was broken in two."

The captain's assessment was right. The vessel went under and disappeared forever. Fortunately, all of the crew made it safely to shore on the ice.

Something that warrants mentioning is the constant need to gather firewood to feed the voracious appetites of the steamers. This was not a problem on a regular run because they hired woodcutters during the winter months to stockpile wood at regular intervals along the rivers. But for those vessels venturing into new territory, it often presented problems. Many hours were spent gathering driftwood off bars along the waterways. The woodcutting was a godsend to the pre-emptors living along the waterways, though, as it gave them a much-needed source of income. Several Prince George pioneers, such as Bill Bellos, got their start in the Interior by cutting wood for the steamers.

Another steamer that took to the river in 1909 was the *City of Quesnel.* A poor performer, it was lengthened and renamed *Quesnel.* Always considered a bit of a dog in the water, it had a spotty career, though in fairness it must be said that it moved a lot of pioneers into the area and had many claims to fame, including bringing the first Caucasian woman into South Fort George.

Throughout its years of service, the *Quesnel* had several run-ins with rocks along the rivers. One of the more pronounced occurred in the Giscome Rapids, when the vessel had over a dozen holes punched through her hull. Efforts to keep her afloat failed but the able crew managed to refloat her at a later date. Many different types of patches were used in emergencies—slabs of bacon, parts of bear hides or even pieces of clothing—whatever it took to get the steamers back to where the ship's able carpenters and engineers could quickly get them back

Steamer *Chilco* lining up Isle de Pierre Rapids in 1909. BC Archives I-33953

into service, often within a matter of hours. The *Quesnel* was retired in 1915, but it would later be returned to service, as we shall see.

During the winter of 1909–1910 the steamer *B.X.* was being built at Soda Creek to put on the Fort George run. When the stern wheel and propeller shafting was being hauled in over the Cariboo Road, an Asian man who knew the Fort George Canyon observed, "Boat never go through canyon, just white elephant!"

This was a palatial vessel 127 x 29 feet, with first-class staterooms and electric lights. It was designed to carry a hundred tons of freight and up to 130 passengers on its two trips per week between Soda Creek and Fort George. Under the competent control of Captain Browne it quickly gained fame.

In an article written for the *Prince George Citizen* in its May 26, 1938, edition, pioneer J.D. Moore recalled:

The writer had the pleasure of being on the steamer *B.X.* on its first trip through the Fort George Canyon on June 24, 1910. It was usual for steamboats to line up through this canyon, so Captain Browne made the necessary arrangements. When the boat was at the most critical point in the canyon, the tree that the line was attached to fell into the river. First Mate Reid (who formerly was in charge of a passenger boat operating into Vancouver) ordered the cable rack thrown into the river, and James Cannon, extra stage driver, tried to sever the cable with an axe. The captain ordered full steam ahead, and the steamer *B.X.* showed she was mistress of the Fort George Canyon. She never lined that canyon again. Moccasin telegraph [runners or canoeists] had informed the citizens of South Fort George that the *B.X.* was coming so when the boat docked, the banks were covered with people who had come ahead. History was made for the north.

The result of this feat was that the epithet "White Elephant" was dropped and "Queen of the North" rightfully took its place. Captain Browne was so skilled at his chosen profession that people used to say they could set their watches when the steamer *B.X.* came in sight because it was always right on time.

The hazards faced by these steamers was brought home with a bang in late September when the B.X. attempted to move a load of freight up to the Hammond townsite on the Nechako River. Right at the mouth of the Nechako it ran aground on a sandbar. Three hours were spent in running a line ashore and winching the good boat off the bar. The *Tribune* newspaper, situated in South Fort George, was always at war with the Hammond townsite newspaper, the *Fort George Herald*, which was located in Central Fort George. Unable to resist taking a shot at the rival townsite and its newspaper, the *Tribune* editor sarcastically noted on October 1:

> Since the accident, however, no attempt has been made to depart from the trodden path of the Fraser—where South Fort George is located—and no more trips will be made to the Hammond monastery up the noiseless Nechako. Awfully sad.

Though it was almost all work and no play for the steamers, there were some exceptions. On one memorable trip the B.X. carried a hundred tons of liquor upriver from Quesnel to Fort George. Among the spirits were champagne, whiskey, rum, beer and just about any other libation a boozer could possibly crave. What made the trip so remarkable was the knowledge that there would be no scarcity of booze in Fort George for some time to come.

Sternwheeler *B.X.* under construction at Soda Creek, 1909–1910. BC Archives 00197

Another exciting trip was the excursion made from South Fort George to Quesnel on September 2, 1911. That's when the B.X. left with a ball team and an abundance of supporters on what turned out to be a fun day for all involved.

Barely one month after her fight with the sandbar, the B.X. got in trouble when it ran onto some rocks at Hudson's Bay Gardens, five miles downriver of South Fort George. On October 8, 1910, Quesnel's *Cariboo Observer* wrote:

> The steamer B.X. is still in such condition that she cannot resume her run on the Fraser. The latest reports received from canoe parties that have arrived from the north are that the vessel is being taken out on temporary ways built on the shore where she grounded last week. The extent of the damage to the hull has not yet been determined but it is thought that several bulkheads were torn open by the force of the collision with the sunken rocks and that it will be some time before she can be repaired. Meanwhile, express matter and mail will go between Quesnel and Soda Creek by stage and automobile.

On October 15 the *Herald* noted:

> On her return trip last week the steamer B.X. struck a rock and sustained severe damage to her hull. Captain Browne beached the boat with three feet of water in one of her compartments. The passengers went on to Quesnel in one of the lifeboats.
>
> It was found necessary to blow out a boulder that lay between the B.X. and the shore in order that repairs could be made to the boat in shallow water, and in doing this work too much powder was used, which resulted in the smashing of most of the glass in the vessel. The exceptionally low water is responsible for this accident to the boat, which has given South Fort George such an excellent service all the past season, and it is to be hoped that the damage can be speedily repaired in order that a few more trips can be made before the close of navigation.

The *Cariboo Observer* continued the story on October 15, 1910:

The steamer *B.X.* arrived at the dock in Quesnel just before noon yesterday and is now being repaired on the temporary ways at the landing. Dan McPhee has charge of the repair work and it is likely the steamer will be in commission again before next weekend.

It was a difficult task for Captain Browne to bring his boat back through the Fort George Canyon on account of the low water and high wind prevailing. Yet the feat was accomplished with the exercise of considerable skill, and she is safe in port again, though with at least two bulkheads on the starboard side badly injured by the encounter with the rocks in the channel above the Fort George Canyon, two weeks ago.

As soon as the *B.X.* struck she began to fill, and had the boat not been built with watertight compartments, the result no doubt would have proved more serious. As it was, the captain was enabled to beach his boat on the east bank of the river, and in a few days she was drawn out of the water sufficient to make the temporary repairs necessary to bring the boat to Quesnel. Mr. Hedon's services were used in blasting out a rock on the bank of the river the second day, which was preventing the boat being skidded out on the shore. The blast was effective, but the force of it shattered practically all the windows on the port side of the cabins.

The *B.X.* will probably run hereafter only between Soda Creek and Quesnel, unless the water rises again. The river, until three days ago, has been rising gradually, but has again fallen some four inches since Wednesday.

It is not surprising that these vessels got in trouble from time to time; the miracle is that they were able to function at all in the low water levels of October.

Some lighthearted entertainment got underway in July 1914, when two steamers decided to have a race. On July 18 the *Herald* carried this brief note:

Passengers arriving on the Royal Mail Steamer *B.X.* on Monday last, report having an exciting race with P. Welch's steamer *Conveyor* on the previous day. The captains of the *B.X.* and *Conveyor* had agreed to an hour's race after leaving Soda Creek, on each side of the river. In spite of making three landings with mail during the race, the *B.X.* was in the lead at Alexandra ferry where the race ended. The *B.X.* arrived here early Monday, having the satisfaction of carrying a broom at masthead, while the people of South Fort George had still greater pleasure of getting their mail several hours ahead of schedule time.

Some sources state that the captain of the *Conveyor* was so upset with losing the race that he rammed the *B.X.* at one point. That story does not fit well with what happened a month later in August 1914, when the *B.X* hit a rock seven miles upriver of Quesnel. A hole was punched in her side, allowing water to pour into one of the compartments. Luckily the *Conveyor's* sister ship *Operator* came along and there were obviously no hard feelings, because she pulled the *B.X.* off the rock. A few days later it was back in service.

The *B.X.* served faithfully through 1915 supplying the railroad construction camps and points south. It was not launched again until May 1918, assisted by a government mail subsidy in order that it could serve settlers along the river south of Prince George who were dependent on the steamers because the promised railroad (PGE) had not materialized.

The *Prince George Citizen* took note of a strange event aboard the *B.X.* in its paper dated August 9, 1918:

Roping a full-grown black bear from the deck of a steamboat was an experience of the *B.X.* deckhands yesterday, according to arrivals from downriver. The bear was seen crossing the river when the steamboat rounded a bend, and coming up alongside the swimming animal one of the deckhands threw a looping rope, which landed squarely over Bruin's head. Then the fun commenced. The rope had slipped down around the middle of the bear, and amid tremendous thrashing and growling Mr. Bear was hauled through the lower gangway to the deck. Picking up an axe, one of the men aimed a blow at Bruin's cranium while the others held fast to the rope. Bruin sidestepped the blow and countered with a left hook that grazed the side of the deckhand's face, inflicting a nasty mark. The bear had risen on his hind legs and was aiming a haymaker at the dazed deckhand when another of the crew landed with the axe on Bruin's skull and he dropped to the deck. Bear steaks figured large on the B.X. bill last night.

One of the game wardens commented that bears had to have a charmed life to gain old age along the river during railway construction, such were the ravenous appetites of the meat-hungry crews.

The romantic days of the B.X. were numbered, though, when she was brought back into action in 1918. She served until August 1919, when she sank after striking a rock near Woodpecker, downriver from Fort George Canyon. She was carrying a hundred tons of cement when she went down. With the B.X. out of service, her sister ship the BC Express was pulled from retirement. After sitting on the riverbank for several years it had dried out, but it was re-caulked and returned to service. Prince George pioneer Gus Lund remembers riding on the

BRITISH COLUMBIA EXPRESS CO.
Steamer Service
STEAMER B.X.
South Fort George to Soda Creek

Semi-weekly leaving Steamer Landing, South Fort George, Tuesdays and Fridays at 7 a.m. arriving Soda Creek at 6 p.m. the same days.

RETURNING—leave Soda Creek 7 p.m. on Tuesdays and Fridays, arriving South Fort George Thursdays and Sundays at 6 p.m.

One of the final advertisements for the palatial *B.X.* was carried in the *Prince George Citizen* on July 26, 1918.

BC Express and seeing the sunken *B.X .*on his trip to Quesnel in late 1919.

Emergency repairs were made to the *B.X.* on-site, but winter arrived and forced operations to be postponed until spring 1919. The return of the *B.X.* to South Fort George the following spring was noted in the *Prince George Citizen:*

A clever feat of seamanship, if river navigation may be so termed, was accomplished by Captain O.F. Browne, the veteran sternwheel captain of the BC Express Company's boats, who towed the disabled steamer *B.X.* into the port at South Fort George on Wednesday last, bringing her safely through the Fort George Canyon lashed alongside his boat. The steamer *B.X.*, which is the pioneer boat of the large class on the upper Fraser, was wrecked at the point above Canyon creek, 30-odd miles below the Fort George Canyon, on August 30th last year. The boat was southbound at the time with about 70 tons of cement aboard for the abutments of the Deep Creek Bridge. She struck a submerged rock and although the shock was slight it was soon noticed that the boat was badly hulled, and before she could be properly beached, the bulkheads gave way in her hull and she settled on the bottom. Later she was lightened and drawn to the riverbank.

The salvage work has been in the hands of the pioneer shipbuilder, Dan McPhee, who built both the *B.X.* and her sister ship and rescuer, the *BC Express.* Repair work was completed on Sunday last and the *BC Express* took hold of the wrecked boat on the evening of that day and commenced the journey upstream. The towed boat was lashed by the side of the *Express* and on reaching the Fort George Canyon the latter boat continued through alone, placed her line, dropped back down the canyon and picked up her tow. Then for the first time in the history of sternwheel boats, one of those craft towed another through a canyon. At a point where the old *Charlotte* was totally wrecked years ago, at the south end of the steamboat channel, steam dropped for a few moments on the *Express'* boilers and "things got pretty lively" as Captain

Browne put it. There was also some trouble at the eddy at the upper end of the steamboat channel, but inch-by-inch the sternwheeler fought her way through the canyon, full steam ahead and with her captain winding in the bowline, until with her disabled sister she gained the free water at the canyon head.

The Fort George Canyon is bad water. Many mishaps have occurred there to steamboats. On the western side of the canyon there stands the cross, erected by one of the pioneer missionary priests where, years ago, a number of Indians who were taking him downriver were drowned.

Tied side by side the two boats almost completely blocked the narrow sections of the steamboat channel. The feat is a singularly able demonstration of river craft on the part of Captain Browne, his officers and crew, and it marks a new departure in the work of sternwheel boats.

As it turned out, an enormous amount of money was spent on the B.X., which was never recouped because the "Queen of the North" was hauled out on the ways at South Fort George, where forty thousand dollars was spent rebuilding her. She served along the lower river for a short time during 1920, but the glamour had gone out of the

The *B.X.*, sunk near Woodpecker. BC Archives A-09848

sternwheelers. On November 9, 1920, the *B.X.* returned to Prince George for the last time. Its upriver trip from Quesnel had taken three days because there was a strike, and when that was settled the boiler sprang a leak. The following day the *B.X.* was pulled out on the ways for the last time and totally dismantled. Its machinery and boiler were shipped to the Mackenzie River for use in other steamers.

In retrospect, many people insisted that when all was said and done the *B.X.* had been correctly named when it was dubbed the "Queen of the North" because she served faithfully for so many years.

Two more steamers were brought into service during 1910. They were the little *Fort Fraser* and the *Chilcotin*—134 x 24 feet—both ships owned by the Fort George Timber and Trading Company. The *Chilcotin* had twenty-two staterooms, each containing two berths, as well as two family staterooms with upper and lower berths. It was built to offer competition to the *B.X.* on the Soda Creek run, while the *Fort Fraser* was to run the Nechako and Stuart Rivers and the upper Fraser River. With its thirteen-inch draft, it was able to travel the shallow waterways, which it did with mixed success.

During the month of August 1910 the little *Fort Fraser*—piloted by Captain Bonser—got into an accident near Tête Jaune Cache that put her out of service for a short time. Two months later on another run to Tête Jaune she ran onto some rocks in the Giscome Rapids and

The steamer *Fort Fraser* in Sestino (Upper White Mud) Rapids on the Nechako River, May 1911. BC ARCHIVES I-33914

badly damaged her hull and some of her machinery. Emergency repairs were made on-site and then she managed to hobble back to Soda
Creek where she was beached for a time. After four years of off-and-
on service the little *Fort Fraser* was pulled out on the ways and placed
on a new hull. As shipping regulations did not permit two keels to be
named alike, the new vessel was renamed the *Doctor*, in honour of Dr.
J.K. McLennan, an officer of the company.

After being refitted, it was described as a neat little vessel, and
the only boat on the upper river that possessed two decks. Built on
the shovelnose design, it was sixty-five feet in length with a beam of
sixteen feet. Just like many of the other steamers, the *Doctor* ended its
service in 1914. It faded into obscurity lying on Pierre Roi Island, just
downriver from South Fort George.

As for the *Chilcotin*, it proved to be no match for the B.X., which
kept up its two-trips-per-week schedule between Soda Creek and Fort
George unless held up by low water levels. Vastly overrated, the *Chilcotin*
had trouble making one trip per week and had to be lined through the
canyons and rapids. In late August 1910 she was on a trip to Fort George
when she was hit with bad luck. Quesnel's *Cariboo Observer* noted:

A most sad accident, resulting in the death of Charlie Land,
occurred during the trip of the *Chilcotin* to Fort George this
week. The body of the young man was brought to Quesnel on
the *Chilco* last evening, accompanied by the bereaved father
who, upon learning of the accident, went up on the B.X.
Wednesday . . .

The unfortunate accident to this popular young man
took place at Fort George Canyon. Land and his partner were
assisting the *Chilcotin* to line ashore. Both bow and stern line
had been secured and Land was at the bowline. The stern line
was thrown off by his partner, permitting the boat to swing
around. He called to Land to "look out and run" as the tree to
which the other line was attached was falling. Land ran, but
in the confusion ran under the falling tree that crushed out
his life. Land was well known and liked in Quesnel where he
and his father had previously taken a contract cutting wood
along the river.

On her return trip from Fort George the *Chilcotin* was heading downriver when she struck a rock near Fort George Canyon.
Apparently a side current caught the vessel and rammed it against a
rock reef. On examination it was found that flaws in the iron of the
hog chains were responsible for the serious damage that ensued. She
was examined and pulled from service for the rest of the season.

Some of the bad press given the *Chilcotin* may have resulted because its owner was the Fort George Timber and Trading Company,
located up the Nechako River at the Hammond townsite. Another
and perhaps unbiased view was carried in the *Herald* on November
4, 1911:

> The Fort George Timber and Trading Co. are certainly to
> be congratulated upon the termination of a most successful
> season. But especially must they be congratulated upon the
> commendable work of Captain D.H. Foster, of their big steam-
> er *Chilcotin*, and his engineers and crew, who have successful-
> ly navigated the staunch riverboat so far into the season. The
> *Chilcotin* arrived here early in the week with a large cargo and
> a considerable number of passengers. The water was excep-
> tionally low and navigation consequently a hazardous matter.
> The company intends to send the boat to Soda Creek again
> to install some new machinery on the ways, if the present soft
> spell continues for a few more days. At present Captain Foster
> and the crew of the *Chilcotin* are upriver making temporary
> repairs to the little steamer *Fort Fraser*, which is beached near
> the Giscome Rapids as the result of an accident that damaged
> her hull and she is expected here early next week.

The captain of the *Chilcotin* pushed his luck a bit too far the following season by working when the river was too low. In fact at one
point during the 1912 season both the B.X. and the *Chilcotin* were out
of service at the same time after striking rocks along the lower river.
On September 28, 1912, the *Fort George Weekly Tribune* stated:

> The steamer *Chilcotin*, of the Fort George Timber and
> Trading Company, ran on a rock on her last trip downstream,

and is now out of the water at Quesnel undergoing necessary repairs. After the accident to the BC Express Company's
steamer B.X., which hit the rocks a few miles south of here a
few weeks ago, the *Chilcotin* was the only connecting link for
river traffic between Fort George and the outside. When she
too went out of commission the prospect for water supplies
was extremely poor. The river freight service is tied up at the
most important season of the year, when the Fraser is falling
for its final closing and the freighters are waiting for snow to
haul the loads straight through from Ashcroft to this point.

I have travelled the Fraser River a great deal and I know just how
difficult it can be to negotiate the waterway in late fall, even with
a small riverboat. It seems almost impossible to me that these giant
steamers sometimes ran through into November. I know they did it,
though, and so these captains have my complete admiration and respect. The ship's carpenters certainly knew their stuff, because they
always managed to get them back into service in short order unless
there was severe damage to the hull.

The dangers facing the steamers were constant no matter
how much care was used, as shown when the *Chilcotin* had a near-
catastrophic accident in late July 1913. It had just entered the
White Mud (Bar) Rapids on the Nechako River when a piston head
blew. Only by the greatest luck—and perhaps a greater amount of
skill—was the vessel saved from disaster. It was a perilous journey
getting it back to South Fort George for repairs. After what some
called "a spotty career" the *Chilcotin* was retired from service at the
close of the 1914 season.

Three more steamers joined the fray in 1912. The most famous
was the *BC Express*, which held the Royal Mail contract and ran a
weekly scheduled service to Tête Jaune Cache. This vessel had a four-
teen-inch draught, making it ideal for the shallow upper Fraser River.
It was 140 feet long, with a 28-foot beam. It had a 265-horsepower
motor and could carry 150 passengers and 110 tons of freight. Its first
journey upriver to the Grand Canyon was recorded in the *Herald* on
July 13, 1912:

The steamer *BC Express* returned from her initial trip upriver on Monday last, completing the 200-mile journey and handling a large quantity of freight in two and a half days. The new steamboat negotiated the lower Grand Canyon without any difficulty. She streamed through the whirlpool and up into the lake that divides the canyon in two without the aid of any lines. A considerable party of businessmen from this place made the trip to the canyon, and all express delight with the showing made by the latest addition to the river fleet. Mr. Charles Miller of Toronto, principal owner of the BC Express Co. was on board. Mr. Miller is very well pleased with the new boat.

On this trip the new boat picked up sixty-five tons of supplies, which it delivered to contractor Sam Magoffin at the mouth of the Willow River.

The only record I found of this vessel being damaged was an occurrence in September 1914. The river was exceptionally low but the *BC Express* attempted to continue working. After pushing her luck on several trips, she finally found a resting place atop several boulders at Hudson's Bay Gardens, where serious damage was inflicted to her hull. She was pulled from service and in three short weeks engineer Dan McPhee completed all repairs, including the big task of re-caulking.

Captain Bucey usually made the 315-mile trip upriver to Tête Jaune Cache in four days and the return trip in two days. On one of his downriver trips he set the record by arriving at Fort George in only forty-two hours. When one realizes that the ship was tied up during the hours of darkness, this was an amazing accomplishment.

Captain Bucey earned the respect afforded him in more ways than one. For instance, there was the time his purser was having trouble getting a passenger to pay his fare. The good captain realized what was happening, so he whispered a message into the purser's ear, and then continued on his way. A moment later a loud scream was heard followed by a shout, "Man overboard!"

Sure enough, the purser—a big man by any standard—had thrown the non-paying passenger into the mighty Fraser! With a good deal of effort the ejected passenger managed to fight his way to shore, and from that point on Captain Bucey's passengers paid their fares without hesitation.

Another memorable event that took place on the BC Express occurred when a card game was in progress. When the money in the pot reached a worthwhile size a policeman stepped forward and showed his badge. Gambling was illegal at the time, so the policeman took the money and returned to his cabin. When one of the ship's officers reported the event to Captain Bucey the captain thought for a moment and then explained to his officer that the policeman had no authority on his vessel. He then told the officer to go to the policeman and offer to split the pot with him. The policeman agreed and the trap was sprung. When the BC Express returned to Fort George Captain Bucey related the events to the policeman's commanding officer and the policeman was on the next steamer heading south.

Captain Bucey's prowess as a riverboat captain was greatly respected. His knowledge of wild water was considerable and he proved his worth by running the Goat Rapids, the Grand Canyon and the seven-mile stretch of the Giscome Rapids without serious mishap. Along with the other steamers, the BC Express served south of Fort George during 1914 and then it was retired for lack of business.

After the wreck of her sister ship the B.X. in 1919, the BC Express was refurbished and served in her place for a short time. The last trip of the season for the BC Express is recorded in the Herald dated October 19, 1919:

The steamer BC Express left for Quesnel Saturday morning with another 90-ton cargo of freight. Considerable difficulty was encountered in making the downriver journey owing to the heavy load and low stage of water but she eventually landed her cargo without mishap.

This is the last trip of the big boat this season, as ice is already running in the river. About 50 tons of freight remains for Cariboo points, but this will probably be taken over the road. Merchants of the lower country may consider themselves fortunate in securing late delivery of so large a quantity of merchandise under prevailing navigation conditions. The BC Express has one more contract on hand for this season—that of releasing the big steamer B.X. from the bar at Woodpecker where she struck several weeks ago.

The BC Express didn't get back to South Fort George for the winter; instead it got caught in the ice at freeze-up and spent the season in a slough near the Blackwater River. The following spring, undamaged, it took up the south run again. This vessel served the Soda Creek run again during 1920, when it was noted:

The fact that the traveller bound for Vancouver may now leave here on the steamer BC Express and arrive in Vancouver in about 40 hours is very little known. Nevertheless the PGE [Railway] steel-head at Deep Creek, five miles south of Soda Creek is in touch with the southern terminal of the steamboat run, by motor cars, and the through journey to Vancouver is possible under favourable circumstances in the total time of 40 hours.

While this time schedule would have raised cheers a few years earlier, the novelty of the sternwheelers had worn off along the upper Fraser River. And so the BC Express, along with its sister ship, B.X., were pulled out on the ways in South Fort George. In November 1920, the manager of the BC Express Company, Willis West, returned to take charge of dismantling both steamers. Their boilers, engines and fittings were removed and shipped to northern Alberta, where they were reassembled on new hulls for use on the Mackenzie River and Lake Athabasca. The abandoned hulls of the two proud ships sat on the riverbank in South Fort George for several years until they were washed away during a period of exceptionally high water.

In order to impart some idea of the amount of freight moved by these steamers, I will give some totals for the B.X. during the summer of 1918: 1,164 tons of steel rails, 276 tons of farm produce, 293 tons of general merchandise, as well as countless passengers.

As it turned out, the faithful service of these sister ships was not rewarded, for not only had the BC Express and the B.X. lost up-river work when the low-level bridges were installed but they also got cheated on their mail contracts. With the arrival of so many thousands of workers and homesteaders into the Interior, the volume of mail had increased tenfold in a few years. Since no allowance was made to increase the contract amount, the BC Express Company took a financial beating.

To further add insult to injury, the Department of Agriculture in Ottawa had advertised that free samples of oats for seeding, as well as several other types of seeds, would be sent to any post office in Canada. The only cost to the receiver was the postage. Each sample of oats weighed five pounds, which meant a postage charge of twenty cents. On the other hand, when oats could be purchased, they were twelve cents a pound in Fort George. This meant that an enormous amount of seed had to be delivered by the Express Company into the Fort George area without payment. At one time there was an accumulation of fifty tons of oat samples in Ashcroft intended for delivery. All told, the Express Company lost over $26,000 in 1913. This would equal over $1 million today.

The other two steamers that were launched in early 1912 were the *Conveyor* and the *Operator*. Both were 142 x 35 feet, with a gross

The *Operator* was taken out of service temporarily to repair damage caused by a falling tree. BC Archives A-01528

weight of seven hundred tons each. These two vessels had served faithfully on the Skeena River, where the good ship *Operator* suffered a serious accident when a tree fell across her stern. As was usually the case, it didn't take long until the engineers and carpenters had her back in service.

In 1911 the railhead reached Hazelton from the west. No longer needed, these two big ships steamed to Vancouver, were dismantled and shipped to Tête Jaune by way of Edmonton, where they were rebuilt during the winter of 1911–12. These vessels were so large that a portion of the riverbank had to be removed so they could negotiate a sharp curve near Tête Jaune. The big ships did yeoman service for FW&S along the upper river during 1912–13. Their ability to each carry two-hundred-ton loads was put to great use in moving vast quantities of supplies as well as loaded scows downriver to the off-loading points. Finally in August 1913 the construction of the low-level bridges barred their access upriver. During their stint on the upper Fraser River only the *Operator* suffered a near-fatal accident. The story was carried in the *Herald* of July 13, 1912:

> The steamer *Distributor* [should be *Operator*] owned by FW&S, engaged in distributing contractors' supplies on the upper Fraser River, was disabled in the Goat River Rapids last week, according to advices brought here by the steamer *BC Express* early in the week.
>
> It appears that the big freight boat struck a rock sideways whilst running the dangerous rapids below the mouth of Goat River, and punctured her hull. The hog chains, which support the frame of the sternwheel vessel, parted at the impact, throwing the vessel out of her lines and practically breaking her back. In order to save the boat from total destruction the whole cargo was jettisoned. One hundred and twenty-five tons of freight was thrown into the river. The horses that were on board were thrown overboard and compelled to swim ashore where they were looked after. A considerable portion of the freight floated downstream and was recovered at points below the scene of the accident, but all tools and heavy material was lost. After the *Distributor* [*Operator*] was lightened

she was maneuvered out of her dangerous position by Captain Myers, and patched up temporarily, and was then able to proceed back to Tête Jaune Cache where FW&S have a force of carpenters in readiness for such contingencies.

The near-tragedy of the steamer *Operator* in Goat River Rapids and the sinking and lifting of the steamer *Quesnel* in the Giscome Rapids were the only serious steamer accidents in the river above Fort George. This seems strange when one considers the perilous water that was faced in the upper river.

The two huge steamers *Operator* and *Conveyor* first came downriver to Fort George in early June 1913. More than just a little impressed, the *Herald* wrote:

> ... This is the first time the big boats which last year were engaged in moving supplies and machinery between Tête Jaune and the Grand Canyon, have made the 300-mile trip from the end-of-steel to this place. Last winter, whilst the boats were laid up on their ways at Dome Creek, the end-of-steel moved far down the river along the route, which they had supplied for this very work.
>
> The *Conveyor* lay at Carlton's camp on the Nechako River when the writer saw her. On the main freight deck a 70-ton steam shovel was being unloaded in preparation for the work of digging its path across the high bank of the Nechako River west of the Grand Trunk townsite. Across the bow of the boat was a completely assembled "dinky" engine [construction locomotive], and besides the machinery the freight deck had room for thousands of pounds of supplies.
>
> The huge river boats are beautifully kept up and appointed. The big engine room reflected the radiance of the electric lights from the polished steel and brass work, and in the bows the huge locomotive type of boiler supplies steam to the expansion engines.
>
> With these craft navigating the river between here and the end of steel the problem of railway construction appears easier to the people who stand by and watch it, and the

prediction made here this week by Vice President Donaldson of the GTP, that the whistle of their locomotives would be heard here this fall, promises to be fully realized.

Barred from upriver work by the railroad bridges, the *Operator* and *Conveyor* went through major transformations during the winter of 1913–1914. The *Herald* dated May 9, 1914, carried this item:

The steamers *Operator* and *Conveyor* have no competitors as freight handlers. Their immense power enables them to handle 150 tons on deck and 150 tons on scow; the total moving power of these two boats being 600 tons per trip, and

The last advertisement for the steamers *Hammond, Operator* and *Conveyor*, 1914, *Fort George Herald.*

if necessary they can make the Quesnel–Fort George round trip in two days . . .

All these boats have been newly fitted for passenger accommodation during the past winter: new state rooms have been added, new liner apportioned to both the dining saloon and state rooms, the bath rooms refitted, new china and silver given to the dining salon stewards and new decorations made in the bridal chambers. In fact every detail having a bearing on the safety and comfort of the passengers has been gone into, and travellers by this route are assured of everything in the way of home comforts to their taste.

The vast amount of money spent on these two steamers was never returned. The anticipated passengers never materialized. The ships served the construction sites of the Pacific Great Eastern Railway and the Soda Creek run during 1914, but that was to be their last year of operation. After serving faithfully on the Skeena and Fraser Rivers, they were pulled out on the bank of the Nechako River at the FW&S landing in Prince George.

In August 1921 Captain Foster returned to Prince George. He visited the steamers *Operator* and *Conveyor*, which had been purchased by the provincial government in the interim. It must have brought tears to his eyes to see these mighty steamers decaying and forgotten after the proud service they had provided. On March 21, 1929, the *Citizen* carried this note in regard to these steamers and the mill at Island Cache:

The boilers for the new mill are those taken out of the PGE steamers *Conveyor* and *Operator*, vessels which were used in the transport of material and supplies along the Fraser River in the construction days of the GTP Railway. For years the old vessels have been decked at the Cache [Prince George] and their boilers were the last of the values to be removed from them. It is fitting that, having contributed so much in the way of opening up the country, they should be continued in the chief industry which has been developed.

Looking back over the years of faithful service given by these two huge ships, one memory stands head and shoulders above all the others, a story told by Willis West, manager of the BC Express Company. On a visit to the Grand Canyon in 1913, he witnessed a most unforgettable sight: the steamer *Conveyor* under full power hurtling down through the upper canyon, her decks crammed with hundreds of construction workers heading for a few days of hellraising at the famous Northern Hotel in South Fort George.

These two proud old steamers spent their last years on the bank of the Nechako River being used as a playground for children; even in death they gave of themselves.

The last steamer to be built on the upper Fraser was the *Robert C. Hammond*, a small oak-ribbed vessel built in Fort George. Launched in 1913, it made a bit of money that year moving supplies along the rivers. With the upper river blocked by bridges, the *Hammond* joined the *Operator* and *Conveyor* serving the Prince George–Soda Creek run and the PGE Railway during 1914, its last year of service.

By 1915 the Prince George area suffered an economic downturn when the construction workers left the area and many young men went to war.

Though hard times befell the steamer companies, they had achieved their objective: people suddenly believed that they had a future in the Interior. Hordes had flocked into the area during the period 1909–1913. Many of the new arrivals were stunned to find that the prime pieces of property had already been snapped up.

With the cancelling of the mail subsidy in 1920 it appeared that steamer service on the upper Fraser had seen its last days, but not so. The steamer *Quesnel*, which had often been held in reserve as an emergency vessel, was given a second chance at life. It was the last steamer to work the upper Fraser River, which it did for a time during 1921. It was co-owned by Captain Foster and W. Matheson, who purchased the vessel with the dream of continual steamer service along the river. The *Prince George Citizen* of February 22, 1921, noted:

That the Fraser River will be navigated for years yet is the belief of Captain D.H. Foster, who has recently pur-chased the sternwheel boat *Quesnel* from the Vancouver-Quesnel Navigation Company. With the vanishing of the BC Express Company's boats from the bosom of the upper Fraser River the belief that the old days of the wheelbarrow boats was gone became general. It is pleasant, therefore, to note the advent of Captain Foster, the pioneer captain of these waters, who contradicts the idea flatly, and backs his judgment by buying a boat and organizing his own naviga-tion company.

. . . During the war Captain Foster was navigating the Tigris, and other strange and tropical rivers, where shallow-draught boats were employed by the Allies in establishing communication for the armies, engaged in ferreting out the enemy. Captain Foster intends to give the boat a thorough overhauling, and to improve the model to some extent. He plans to fit her up in the best manner possible, and to es-tablish a semi-weekly freight and passenger service on the river. Associated with Captain Foster in his enterprise is W.J. Matheson of South Fort George, a veteran purser of the upper Fraser River boats.

Captain Foster is the pioneer captain of the upper Fraser. He was captain of the old *Charlotte* built in 1900 [1896] by the late Senator Reid. This boat met her doom on a bar below the Fort George Canyon some years ago when she went to pieces after grazing the canyon wall. Later the captain piloted the *Chilcotin* and *Hammond*.

The two men spent the greater part of their life savings on repair-ing the *Quesnel*, which had lain discarded on the riverbank at South Fort George for about seven years. After launching, she made a couple of successful trips downriver before she finally met her end in Fort George Canyon. The *Citizen* of May 13, 1921, noted:

An account of the wreck indicates that the current has changed in some manner in the canyon. The boat was threading her way across the upper end of the canyon to get to the low-water passage when it went aground on the smooth reef, which lies at the head of the canyon, above the litter of rock islands which break it up into the many passages. "It seemed impossible to keep her off," Captain Foster states, and after 20 years experience on inland waters, many of which have been spent on the upper Fraser, the captain lost his first boat when the *Quesnel* went on the reef. The rising water has driven the boat farther and farther on the rocks and in her present position it seems impossible to get her off.

A week later, on May 20, the *Herald* added:

The hull of the sternwheeler, which lies on an island in the Fraser about a half-mile below South Fort George [Pierre Roi Island], is now being prepared for the reception of the machinery of the disabled steamer *Quesnel*, which came to grief a fortnight ago in the Fort George Canyon. Captain Foster and the crew of the *Quesnel* are hard at work removing the

MOTOR BOAT ROUNDER

The Fastest Boat on the River
Plying Between South Fort George
and Quesnel
Carrying His Majesty's Mail, Passengers,
Express and Freight
Leaves South Fort George Wednesday and
Saturday at 8 a.m. Arrives Quesnel 9 p.m.
Leaves Quesnel—Thursday and Sunday
Mornings. Arriving at South Fort George
same day.

A motorboat *Rounder* advertisement in the *Prince George Citizen*, 1921.

paddlewheel and machinery of the disabled vessel and it is intended to have the *Doctor* take up the river run at an early date.

Several days were spent in unloading the hundred kegs of beer and a car that were on the deck of the damaged *Quesnel*. When repairs were finally completed the intent was to put the vessel in the water and move it up to Pierre Roi Island, where the machinery was to be transferred to the *Doctor*. Once the *Quesnel* was moved out from shore, it rolled over and slid beneath the water to its final resting place. It was a sad ending to yet another of the proud steamers that bravely faced the canyons and rapids along the turbulent river.

The final blow to the steamers, however, was the cancellation of the PGE Railway in 1921 due to a lack of funds.

In a desperate attempt to stay in the transportation business, Captain Foster and W. Matheson purchased the old meat boat from Pat Burns. This boat had seen better days after plying the upper river for many years, but it was still capable of carrying many tons of freight and passengers. Named the *Circle W.*, it was put on the Prince George–Quesnel run hauling passengers and freight in 1921.

After the steamer whistles were no longer heard along the upper Fraser River, three gasoline-powered boats—the *Rounder*, the *Viper* and the *Circle W.*—continued hauling passengers and freight between Prince George and Soda Creek. Two of these boats were still in operation in the summer of 1921, and the *Rounder* worked the run until 1925 under the competent control of Jimmie Williams. As it turned out, 1921 was the year that the upper Fraser River said goodbye to the last of the dozen steamers that worked between Tête Jaune Cache and Soda Creek, 472 miles (760 km) downriver. The steamers were: *Enterprise, Victoria, Charlotte, Quesnel, Fort Fraser* (renamed *Doctor*), *Nechacco* (renamed *Chilco*), *B.X., Chilcotin, BC Express, Operator, Conveyor* and *Robert C. Hammond.*

After fifty-eight years of service, the romantic days of the fifteen million (today's currency) dollars' worth of sternwheelers on the upper river were over, their whistles replaced by the whistles of steam locomotives. Only some half-rotted woodpiles, a few winch pins in the canyons and some abandoned homesteads are left to remind us of how these great vessels so proudly faced the wild canyons and rapids of the upper Fraser.

As for the stagecoaches that worked out of Prince George, I was certainly surprised to learn that Al Young was still running a stage service from Prince George through the Blackwater to Quesnel in 1921. The accompanying advertisement says it all.

PASSENGERS FOR QUESNEL

STAGE SERVICE—Stage leaves
Prince George Hotel every Tuesday
and Friday morning.
For particulars see Al Young, at
Prince George Hotel

EXPRESS TO CARIBOO

This advertisement was in the *Prince George Citizen* of February 22, 1921.

Other Canyons & Rapids

There were many other dangerous spots along the upper river besides the Grand Canyon. The newspapers were full of the tragedies that occurred throughout the early years. Perhaps the earliest recorded fatality occurred at Cottonwood Canyon in 1873 when an official of the Hudson's Bay Company drowned there.

The second most deadly spot along the upper river after the Grand Canyon was the Fort George Canyon, fifteen miles (24 km) downriver from Fort George.

Many years ago the Prince George area was covered by an enormous lake, the Pineview district having been a lake bottom at one time. Eventually the Fort George Canyon washed out, the water level dropped and this spectacular canyon was left.

During the winter of 1909–1910 over $2,500 ($125,000 in today's currency) was spent clearing rocks and obstructions from the canyon. When questioned, one of the workers stated that a channel was cleared to allow boats to go through during high water. This was the equivalent of admitting the money had been wasted, because boats had always been able to go through at high water. The only actual improvements were that a bit of portage trail was cut and four rings placed in the canyon walls for lining the steamers up against the powerful current.

In May 2005 Vern Gogolin of Prince George took Dale Sinclair, Eric Klaubauf and I to this historic canyon in his riverboat for a day of exploration. Along the way we paused at Burntwood Creek, which was renamed Six-Mile Creek by the steamer captains because of its distance from Fort George. Four miles farther downriver another stream emerges from the east. This creek was named Ten-Mile Creek for the same reason.

We spent several hours at the canyon, where we followed the old portage trail around it and found one of the steel pins used to winch the steamers through. I felt humbled contemplating those huge stern-wheelers making their way through the narrow confines of Canoe Pass along the western shore. On the eastern side of the canyon the water still boils over the reef that was never completely removed, where a whirlpool still springs to life during periods of high water.

Perhaps because this canyon was so visible to the travelling public, it got more than its share of media attention, such as the following item from the *Herald* dated September 10, 1910:

Premier McBride had intimated his intention of drawing the attention of the Ottawa authorities to the much needed im-

Sternwheeler *Nechacco* winching up Canoe Pass in Fort George Canyon, 1909.
BC ARCHIVES B-00306

provements required to aid navigation in the Fort George Canyon. The *Victoria Colonist* last week devoted a whole column to editorial comment on this subject. Mr. Lugrin, the *Colonist*'s editor, during his recent visit to this section with Premier McBride's party, was able to realize the situation from personal observation. The *Colonist* draws attention to the constant danger of damage or destruction to boats when passing through this canyon, and shows that the aggregated value of the steamboats now plying on this river is in the neighbourhood of $250,000 [$12.5 million in today's currency], also pointing out that two of the boats are now "hors de combat" from their battles with this menace to life and property.

The writer has passed through the Fort George Canyon in the winter, and has seen the obstructing reef in the eastern channel standing high and clear of the ice. Rock men with steel and powder could remove this reef in sixty days.

The Fort George Canyon marks the very entrance into the Fort George District itself. It is rather a rude surprise to our many visitors from the world's centres of population to be crowded to the after end of a steamboat in order that the stern-wheel may take a greater dip, and from there to watch the boat fighting its way against the mightiest forces of nature through narrow tortuous channels lined by precipitous rock shores, after travellers have read of the wonderful Fraser River navigable for a thousand miles.

The blowing out of the reef in the eastern channel would give a straight deep-water channel for steamboats at any stage of the water. No other work would, we believe, be necessary. The writer has passed through this channel at the extremes of both high and low water, and has observed that were this obstruction removed, much water now deviated through the other channels would flow through the eastern channel which is now too narrow to give passage to more than about fifty per cent of the water passing through the canyon . . .

All the media attention finally bore fruit, because the following winter the eastern reef was reportedly blown away. The desired results were not achieved, though, because as already noted, the Fort George Canyon still proved to be the deadliest obstacle to steamers on the entire Fraser River.

Canoes, dugout or otherwise, were just one of several modes of transportation that were totally inadequate for dealing with the rapids and canyons along the river, as the following story taken from the *Fort George Post* confirms:

> While going down the Fraser River from South Fort George to Quesnel Tuesday morning, E.F.W. Heath, Martin Clarke of the Forestry Branch office, and Provincial Constable Burns were capsized from the canoe in which they were riding just after they had negotiated the worst piece of water on their route—the Fort George Canyon. Mr. Clarke and Mr. Burns lost their lives before assistance could reach them, although they made a valiant fight to reach the riverbank, clinging to the canoe meantime.
>
> Mr. Heath, believing that the canoe would not hold up the three of them, let go and grabbed a roll of blankets, clinging to which he managed to float to shore in the whirling eddies of the swift-running Fraser. After getting to shore, Mr. Heath hurried to assist his comrades but had to make a detour through the trees across a strip of land around which the river took a bend, and before he reached sight of the river his friends had disappeared, and up to this time no trace of the bodies has been discovered.

Back about 1910, a story of tragedy at the Fort George Canyon made the rounds of area newspapers when a raft loaded with Chinese miners supposedly went down with the loss of all lives on board. Some people treated the story as a hoax, saying that most certainly some would have survived the ordeal. About a month later word reached the newspaper offices that these miners were found alive and well, prospecting farther down the river.

Another dangerous spot along the upper river was the seven-mile stretch of the Giscome (sometimes spelled Giscomb or Giscombe) Rapids about thirty-five miles (56 km) upriver from Fort George.

During the years of railway construction it claimed its share of lives, as shown in this story from the *Fort George Herald* on May 20, 1911:

MEETS WATERY GRAVE IN GISCOME RAPIDS

John Macdonell and George Haines left Tête Jaune Cache on May 7th for South Fort George in order to provision up for a prospecting summer they intended making on Goat River and adjacent country. George Haines conducted a stopping place at Moose Lake, known as Mile 27, BC. He sold out his business and supplies and was on his way here to restock. While shooting the Giscome Rapids the canoe he was in swamped, and he was drowned last Wednesday. His partner, John Macdonell, arrived here Thursday morning and reported the matter to the provincial police.

"Haines was no canoe man," said Macdonell, in relating the event, "and of a nervous temperament. We left the Cache in a dugout with limited provisions and going through the Goat Rapids, Haines walked the bank of the river while I took the canoe through. We spent the night of Tuesday at Giscome Portage and after breakfast there Wednesday morning Haines took a walk down to the Rapids—a bad stretch of

Portaging supplies three-quarters of a mile around Fort George Canyon. BC ARCHIVES I-33280

water seven miles long and 23 miles from South Fort George. He covered part of the ground and on returning to camp stated that he saw nothing bad about the water and would go through in the canoe. We both got into the dugout, Haines at the bow. Shortly after entering the rapids, the white foam, the driftwood and the boiling water must have frightened Haines for he stood up in the canoe and caught the edges causing her to rock violently until she took in water and swamped and upturned. We both caught the edges of the canoe, one at either end. Haines was a big man and weighed 220 pounds— 50 pounds heavier than I. The difference in weight kept my end of the canoe further out of water, and all I could see of Haines was the tips of his moccasins on one side and his head on the other, and he was always swallowing water. Haines had gloves on at the time and about halfway through the rapids he let go and disappeared. I managed to upturn the canoe and get on the bottom of it, steering with my feet until I ran against a logjam and partly embedded the canoe. I took to the shore and followed the bank of the river upstream to where I imagined Haines had let go and hunted the vicinity all night, without result. Having been almost all in myself, I concluded to come to South Fort George and report the accident to the police.

Haines was a cook, and a prominent Eagle, and at one time worked in the Victoria Hotel in Edmonton. He was a native of Iowa, and had considerable money on his person at the time of the accident.

Regrettably, I was unable to determine whether or not Haines' body was ever found. Obviously, the considerable amount of money he was carrying must have made him a tempting target for robbers.

On June 8, 1911, the *Herald* again noted:

A third drowning accident, within the past three weeks, occurred here last Tuesday under particularly distressing circumstances. The victim of the capsized dugout was a young Englishman named Harry Baxter, hailing from Shropshire.

The circumstances surrounding the affair which led up to the death are as follows: it appears that Kenneth McKenzie, the millwright, had taken a canoe from town to Pierre Roi's ranch, below the Collins addition. As the water was high along the banks between the ranch and town, he walked back over the trail, the distance being not over half a mile. Wishing to bring the canoe back that evening, McKenzie asked Baxter, whom he knew to be a canoe man, to go down to Roi's place and help pole back. They started from the ranch and made good progress up the shore, though in places there was no poling bottom, and the brush swept far out into the river. At a place near where the first bench on the town-site rises at the water's edge, the overhanging brush prevented them from standing up, and at that point the accident took place. McKenzie was kneeling in the bow pulling the canoe upstream by the brush, whilst Baxter, also kneeling, was trying to get poling bottom in the deep water, when without warning the canoe listed violently and capsized. Finding some hold for his pole, Baxter evidently took advantage of it and his pole slipped and overbalanced him, and precipitated both canoe-men into the river. McKenzie's feet became enmeshed in a mass of brush on the bottom and the canoe turned over on top of him. As the dugout was turning over McKenzie shouted to his companion to hang on to the canoe, anticipating no danger, as he was only eight or ten feet from the shore.

McKenzie made it to shore and immediately went searching downriver. The canoe was found tangled in some willows a short distance downriver, but no trace of the twenty-three-year-old Baxter was found. This makes one wonder how many drowning tragedies would have been prevented if only these rivermen had had access to proper flotation devices.

It should be noted that Pierre Roi—mentioned above—owned a ranch just downriver from South Fort George. An early-day voyageur for the Hudson's Bay Company, he passed on in 1938 at the age of eighty-seven years.

A short distance upriver of Fort George was another danger spot that claimed several lives. The *Herald* of May 31, 1913, carried this headline:

DANGER LURKS IN PATH OF VOYAGEURS

A sad drowning accident, which adds to the list of those whose lives have been surrendered to the treachery of the upper Fraser River, occurred this week at the mouth of the Willow River when two young men—well-known and popular in this section—were wrecked in their canoe on the reef below the Willow and drowned before the eyes of a number of men along the grade. The identity of the victims was at no time in doubt for they were both members of the Green and Burden survey crew named Fred Lucas and Odo Chamberlain . . . No exact details of the accident were forthcoming but eye witnesses on the grade were attracted to the disaster by cries for help after the canoe had overturned and the two men were struggling in the water.

What made the tragedy really hit home was the fact that both men were experienced rivermen as well as property holders in the area. The newspaper went on to attack the government once again for failing to install proper signs above the most deadly spots along the river.

Rocks were not the only hazards, as proved by this event described in the *Fort George Tribune* on May 31, 1913:

Mrs. Helen Skelow, wife of a station-man on the GTP, and an unknown man named Pete were drowned when the raft on which they were riding struck a log jam and was sucked under by the swift current about 10 miles above Fort George. The raft had nine people aboard altogether, three of whom jumped on the jam when the raft struck. The others were thrown in the water and were rescued, as their heads bobbed up between the logs, by the three who were on the jam. The two drowned were never seen again after the raft struck. The entire outfit on the raft was lost as well as their time checks. The survivors were picked off the jam by the steamer *Chilcotin* three hours after the accident and brought to Fort George.

The media kept jabbing away at the government, and finally the *Herald* won a round when they noted:

A mammoth sign bearing a warning to downriver navigators has just been completed for the local mercantile firm of Kennedy, Blair and Co. and will be erected at the head of the Grand Canyon. Beneath the warning "Danger" is painted a map showing the contour of the dangerous channel, the landing and portage, and a completely sketched plan of how to avoid the perilous whirlpool. Had the authorities been possessed of sufficient initiative to erect such a warning before traffic became general on the upper waters, the lives of many inexperienced navigators would not have paid forfeit.

There can be no doubt that the newspaper was right in its analysis. Why the signs had not been erected sooner is a mystery that boggles the mind, for it remains the blackest mark against the GTP during the entire period of railroad construction. This sign, as well as signs above Giscome and Goat River Rapids, were not put in place until late summer 1912—only one year before commercial navigation ceased on the upper river.

And yet again on July 12, 1913, the *Herald* wrote:

The Fraser River claimed another victim in the person of J. Wardner the other day when a scow on which he was employed struck a rock in the Goat Rapids, according to surviving members of the crew who reached South Fort George on Monday night. The ill-fated scow was one of 18 belonging to FW&S, which were being brought under load from Tête Jaune to Fort George. They all got through the rapids safely except the one on which Wardner was working. When he saw that a wreck was inevitable Wardner jumped overboard and was not seen again. The other three occupants succeeded in jumping to another scow to which they were roped, and they afterwards cut the ropes to get free of the wreck . . .

The article went on to state that FW&S recognized the problem and were taking steps to see that at least two experienced rivermen would go out with each scow in the future. The official stated that they had lost over one hundred thousand dollars worth of supplies through the sinking of their scows, which was enough money to buy two large steamboats. He also added that about a hundred scows a day were heading downriver to lower construction camps. These were just FW&S scows; there were also countless other scows heading on to Fort George. Perhaps the number of scow-men on the Fraser during 1913 did equal or surpass the total number of 1,500, as stated in several books. With so many scows running the rapids and canyons it is certainly not surprising that so many lives were lost.

During one of his speeches on early-day scowing, George Williams, the "Wizard of the River" reminisced:

These scows carried between 20 and 30 tons each, and were about 40 feet long, and 12 to 16 feet wide. In high water the trip from Tête Jaune Cache took about five days and in low water, up to 12 days, as they had to be hand-spiked over the shallow bars of the upper river. This operation was called "frogging" and was not at all enjoyed by crews, particularly on frosty mornings. It was a common sight to be drifting down the river and see a scow stuck on a rock in the numerous rapids, with the crews out in the water up to their waists, trying to pry it loose with big poles. The scow crews drifting past were always sympathetic enough to call over and ask how the "frogging" was.

During the hectic period of getting the supplies down to the railway contractors and townspeople from 1910 to 1913 there were wrecked scows piled up on nearly every rock in Goat and Giscome Rapids. Numbers of men made good money salvaging wrecked merchandise from the logjams below. The more thrifty crews just took their scows up a side stream, unloaded and cached the supplies, then went back and reported they had been wrecked.

In working a scow one generally felt better after getting through the Grand Canyon safely. There were approximately 50 men drowned in this canyon in one season. In high water the whirlpools sucked down the scows and crews if you were unfortunate enough to get caught in one of them. During 1913 when scowing reached its height, there were about 1,500 men employed as scow-men or "River Hogs" as they were generally called. They made money fast and spent it faster.

Drifting downstream for 315 miles and then catching the next boat [steamer] back was a dream of paradise come true for most of the "River Hogs." There was not enough state-room accommodation on the steamboats for all the men and some trips they were so crowded that they could not spread their blankets on the decks. Between playing poker, free-for-all fights and scratching lice, a good time was had by all who survived this strenuous game, where life was about as uncertain as it became afterwards in the frontline trenches of the Great War.

Scows on the rocks, c.1912. Northern BC Archives and Special Collections, Parker Bonney Collection, Accession #2003.13.2

It is a fact that finding bodies along the Fraser River became so commonplace that it was barely rated newsworthy. For instance, there was this brief item in the *Herald* of August 23, 1913:

A dead man was found on an island a mile below the town this week [Pierre Roi Island]. He was not identified and was buried by the police. Another case of "found drowned."

Following is a rather bizarre story taken from the *Herald* of January 21, 1914:

Some strange things find their way into print at times. A few weeks ago an Italian labourer in Winnipeg told of a disaster on the Fraser River near this point in which 75 men lost their lives. The Associated Press wired the editor of this paper asking for confirmation or denial of the story. An emphatic denial was sent at once, but in the meantime the yarn had been broadcast over the Associated Press wires, and published in most of the daily papers in Canada. Here it is, clipped from the *Edmonton Capital* of January 6th:

"Suffering from injuries received in a wreck on the Fraser River in which it is claimed 75 men lost their lives, Angelo Pugliese applied at the immigration office yesterday for aid. He came to Canada six months ago, and securing work with the GTP, he was sent with many others to the end of steel in BC. For a time he was kept busy in the vicinity of Fort George, but early in November with 100 other labourers he was sent further west, the trip requiring the party to cross the Fraser River. In spite of the swift-flowing current, something not much feared by experienced rivermen, the entire party was loaded into a large boat for the trip across the river.

"The navigation was difficult; the boat became unmanageable and crashed into a large rock in the centre of the stream. The frail craft was dashed to pieces and the human cargo plunged into the torrent. The greatest confusion prevailed. The strength of the current made swimming impossible and the struggling men were either dashed to death on the rocks or carried to their death by the flood. Of the five score men that boarded the boat, only 25 were taken from the water alive, and many of these were more or less seriously injured. Only five bodies were recovered."

Pugliese was numbered among the injured, having his feet and neck badly injured. He was in the hospital at Edmonton for some time, and when discharged came to Winnipeg. Pugliese stated that no inquiry of any kind had ever been made as to the cause of the accident. Angelo was probably in bad need of aid when he told this story, but it still remains a fact that more "fake" newspaper items appear under a Winnipeg date line than any other in Canada.

The previous story was thankfully bogus, and this becomes obvious when one reads that they went west of Fort George to cross the Fraser River, because there is no Fraser River west of Fort George (Prince George). This story does not in any way diminish the human price paid along the Fraser River for railroad development—it was far higher than we will ever know.

Running downstream in unknown water was the main cause of accidents. Therefore it was important to have at least one experienced riverman on each vessel. Two men learned this lesson the hard way back in July 1914 when they took a canoe through the Giscome Portage on their way to Peace River. On their arrival at Summit Lake they were misinformed about the distance to the Parle Pas Rapids. They encountered the rapids before they expected them, the canoe tipped and both men were thrown into the river. A strong swimmer, A. Haight managed to make it to shore, but his partner Hugh Brown drowned. The *Herald* summarized:

This adds another death to the already fast-growing list of drowning accidents occurring in these fast-flowing rivers, and inexperienced men should never attempt the water route except accompanied by experienced rivermen, and even with these men it is not altogether safe.

The people travelling downriver on rafts were at a decided disadvantage because rafts were so hard to manoeuvre. When rocks or sweeps (trees that stick out into the river) were not seen in time, there was no possibility of avoiding an accident. Such was the case when Mr. C. Oliver, Mr. W.J. Wright and his brother C. Wright were floating down the Nechako River in June 1914. Suddenly their raft struck a sweeper and all three men were flung overboard. Two of them made it to shore but twenty-seven-year-old W.J.Wright was drowned. His brother spent ten long days searching along the river until the body was found.

A great deal of work was performed along the Nechako River in the early years of steamboat travel, with Isle de Pierre (Island of Stone) Rapids receiving the most attention. Another problem spot was the White Mud Rapids, which posed problems to the steamers until a channel was blasted through in 1912–1913. One can still see the steamer's firewood piled on the riverbank just upstream of these rapids. Over ninety years have passed since this wood was cut, but surprisingly some of it is still sound. This rapids' name was changed from Bar Rapids to White Mud Rapids because of the abundant white mud that oozes from its banks.

The Chilako (Mud) River was the location of a fort for many years. In an article published in *British Columbia History*, Vol. 38, No.2, Peter Trower pointed out that the original Fort George, established at the confluence of the Nechako and Fraser Rivers by Simon Fraser in 1807, was abandoned the following year. In 1820 a fort was constructed near the mouth of the Chilako River. It was known as Chala-oo-chick until 1821, when the name was changed to Fort George. This post was moved to what is now Prince George in 1823. In August of that year two of the men in the employ of the fort were murdered and the fort was closed in 1824. It reopened in 1829 and stayed open until 1915. In 1948 a new Hudson's Bay store was established in Prince George, where it remains to this day.

The danger involved in scowing along the rivers was pointed out once again in this story carried in the *Herald* May 30, 1914:

> On Monday of this week a scow of lumber for a Quesnel builder, in charge of Bert Mumpower, struck a rock at the head of

China Rapids about five miles downstream of Hixon Creek, resulting in a total loss. There were 12 men on the scow besides Mumpower. They all managed to get on the rock and were rescued from their perilous position by Captain Foster on the steamer *Hammond*. There is considerable danger in scowing on the lower river, especially on account of the probability of meeting one of the various steamers in either of the canyons. All steamers should give a long warning whistle before they reach the foot of the two canyons, on their up trips, thus giving the scows a chance to get ready.

Proof that even the best rivermen did not escape danger was supplied in June 1914 when the famous river hog George Williams had a scary moment. Along with seven other men, he was moving a scow loaded with four hundred bales of oats when they wrecked just below Fort George Canyon. Apparently a whirlpool caught the scow and simply overpowered the crew, eventually bringing the scow against a rock. The side of the scow was bashed in, but the crew all climbed to safety atop the rock. The steamer *B.X.* happened along four hours later, plucked them off their perches atop the boulder and returned them to South Fort George.

These men were indeed fortunate to have had their accident at a time when the steamers were travelling the river. It appears to me that at least twenty-seven men were rescued off rocks by steamers during the years of GTP construction.

Something that needs mentioning was the danger inherent in travelling on the ice, which was common during railway construction. Countless numbers of horses were lost through the ice during those years. In fact, my sister-in-law's father was employed on the railway, and he lost a team of horses through the ice near where the community of Penny stands today. It was simply an occupational hazard. People who were expert at travelling the rivers on snowshoes in winter had a foolproof method for getting themselves across in safety. They cut a long pole with which they struck the ice ahead of them. If the ice did not break from the impact, then it would certainly hold their weight. For the inexperienced the risk was much higher, as described in the *Fort George Tribune* of November 27, 1909.

According to the story, Joe Boyer and John Porter left their preemptions on the south side of the Fraser and made their way to a point across the river from South Fort George. Since this was late November, the ice had just jammed but had not set up enough for travel. While Mr. Porter waited on the shore, Mr. Boyer took a chance and started across. He had not gone far when he realized it was not safe, so he started back. Almost at once he broke through and got wet up to the armpits. It was after sundown, with the temperature well below zero, but Boyer got back on the ice and made it to shore. By the time he got back on the bank, his partner had a fire going, but whether it would have saved him or not is unknown. Several Fort George Natives witnessed their plight and, being river-wise, they knew the ice jammed tighter farther downriver. They crossed on the safer ice and brought the men back to warmth and safety in Fort George.

A much worse fate awaited three men that were inspecting land in December 1913. Chris Muller, Max Drechler and Frank Schalling had just boarded their boat upstream of Fort George when they ran into an icejam that turned their boat upside down. Only Schalling made it to solid ice, but when he threw a line to one of his friends the current was too strong for him to hold on. After shouting for ten minutes, Schalling's cries were finally heard at Sam Magoffin's construction camp. The workmen came to his rescue and dragged him ashore. Both Drechler and Muller were lost under the ice.

Such was the price paid by many of the pioneers. Their options were limited and constant danger was their lot.

Sometimes accidents happened because of poor decisions. In late 1920 two river hogs attempted to move a large raft of bridge timbers downriver from South Fort George for the Pacific Great Eastern Railway. An agreement had been made that three or four men would be at the landing site to help them tie up the raft on their arrival, but no one arrived. One of the men jumped off the raft with a line but because of the fast current was unable to snub the rope to a tree in order to stop the scow. The rope got away from him and the raft carried on downriver with its helpless occupant praying for a miracle. When it reached Fort George Canyon, the raft shot through at great speed and somehow avoided all the rocks. Several miles farther downriver it finally came to rest on a sandbar near Woodpecker, where the shaken rider managed to get ashore. A few hours later a powerboat came along and gave him a ride back upriver to Prince George.

Life was not all challenge and sorrow for these rivermen. Ted Williams, son of the "Wizard of the River," pointed this out to me when I asked him about early-day humour. Among the memories of stories told by his father was a recollection from a night spent camping along the river, when the scow-men engaged in telling tall tales. Ted's favourite story concerned a man hunting deer during a terrible windstorm. Apparently the man fired at the deer and a powerful gust of wind took the bullet around in a circle, with the result that it came back and passed through the shooter's hat from behind. The bullet then continued on and got the deer on its second pass.

Another tale from Ted's father was about him and his canoe partners bringing a writer downriver, when nature called. They paddled the craft to the shore, where the writer spent a few minutes in the woods. Suddenly there erupted some of the foulest swearing ever heard on the upper river. When the tirade subsided, the fellow emerged from the bushes and told George what had transpired: after he had relieved himself, the would-be woodsman had wiped with some vegetation, which included a devil's club leaf, covered with a countless number of tiny barbs. It is safe to say that that was one mistake that writer never repeated.

Perhaps it should be pointed out that prior to the advent of newspapers in the Interior, toilet paper of any kind was unknown. The choice was simple—vegetation such as moss in summer, and snow in winter. Just imagine using snow at fifty below!

The Railroad

In July 1903 Sir Wilfrid Laurier presented a bill to the House of Commons to incorporate the Grand Trunk Pacific Railway Company. The proposed railway would go through the Yellowhead Pass, down the Fraser River, along the Nechako and Endako Rivers to the Bulkley and Skeena Rivers and then on to the Pacific coast. This route had been chosen by the railway genius Sandford Fleming twenty years earlier on his exploration trip through BC. As history has shown, it was a logical choice.

Originally the GTP was the brainchild of Charles Melville Hayes, who was lost in the *Titanic* disaster of 1912. Had he lived another two years he would have seen his dream come true with the completed railroad stretching from Winnipeg to Prince Rupert, on the west coast of BC. The story of the GTP construction is one of great achievements as well as bitter disappointments, such as the fifteen-day strike in July 1910 that lost the GTP about $1 million ($50 million in today's currency).

As early as 1903 surveyors were at work in the mountains of BC looking for a suitable railway grade. Out of three possible choices, the

Prince Rupert route picked by Fleming was chosen in 1906. Soon a multitude of surveyors were involved in surveying the grade.

To give some idea of what the builders were up against in constructing a railroad through the Rockies, I quote from the book *The Northwest Passage by Land*, written by Viscount Milton and Dr. W.B. Cheadle in 1865:

> In the course of our morning's journey, we were surprised by coming upon a stream flowing to the westward. We had unconsciously passed the height of land and gained the watershed of the Pacific. The ascent had been so gradual and imperceptible, that, until we had the evidence of the water flow, we had no suspicion that we were even near the dividing ridge.
>
> The next afternoon found us encamped at Buffalo-dung Lake . . . The lake consists of two portions. The mountains appeared to rise right out of the water on the further or southern shore of the lake, whilst close behind us, on the northern side, commenced verdant and swelling hills, the bases of loftier heights, which rose further back in many a naked, ragged rock or ice-crowned peak. Two of these on opposite

When surveyors could not get access to dog teams, they pulled their loaded sleds through the forests. Northern BC Archives and Special Collections, Parker Bonney Collection, Accession #2003.13.2

sides of the lake were particularly fine, one to the northwest, the other to the southwest . . . We took the liberty of naming them Mount Fitzwilliam and Mount Bingley.

On the 10th [of July] we struck the Fraser River, sweeping round from the southwest in a narrow gorge, to expand some miles down into Moose Lake. Our route now lay along the north bank of the Fraser, and the travelling was exceedingly difficult and harassing. The river had overflowed its banks up to the almost perpendicular sides of the straightened valley in which it was confined. The track was completely under water up to the horses' girths, and we spent the greater part of the day in wading and the rest in toiling through swamps beset with fallen timber. It was impossible to stop, for there was neither dry place for us to camp nor pasture for the horses, and we therefore travelled on until dark, very thankful to find a place to rest at last. . . . But if this 10th of July was a hard and harassing day, the 11th was still worse . . . Soon after we started we came to Moose River, which was somewhat difficult to ford for the water was high and rapid, pouring over the horses' shoulders in the deepest part.

We reached Moose Lake before noon, and travelled along until dark without finding any resting place. The lake was high, up to the base of which the waters spread. It was again a day of marching through water, and the horses perversely wandered off into the deeps, and floated about, soaking flour and pemmican. Accumulations of driftwood barred the passage along the shore in many places, and we were compelled to scale the mountainsides. Horse after horse rolled back in the attempt and we had to cut off their packs in the water and carry up the loads on our backs, to enable the animals to scramble up the steep ascent. We worked hard in the hope of reaching the end of the lake before dark, but the sun went down when we were several miles distant, and we were compelled to spend the night in a bare sand-pit, where there was not a blade of grass for our tired and hungry animals, who ranged restlessly to and fro until the morning.

Moose Lake is a fine sheet of water, about fifteen miles in length, and not more than three miles in breadth at the widest point . . . On the south side, the hills rose perpendicularly out of the water for perhaps 2,000 feet, beyond which was the usual background of rocky and hoary peaks. Over the edge of this mighty precipice a row of silver streams poured with unbroken fall, the smallest ones dissipated in mist and spray ere they reached the lake below. This beautiful series of cascades we named the Rockingham Falls.

The descent on the western slope was very rapid and continual, although nowhere steep, and a change in the vegetation marked the Pacific side. The cedar, the silver pine, and several other varieties now first appeared, and became more and more frequent . . . The timber was altogether of a larger growth, and the huge trunks, which barred the path, rendered our progress very laborious. The pack horses wearied us by breaking away into the forest rather than leap over the obstructions in the way . . . Then they rushed about in every direction but the right one, crashing and rumbling about the timber, and often involving themselves in most serious embarrassment, jamming their packs between two adjacent trees, trying to pass under an inclining trunk too low to admit the saddle, or jumping into collections of timber where their legs became hopelessly entangled.

On the afternoon of the 13th we came to a place where the trail passed along the face of a lofty cliff of crumbling slate. The path was only a few inches in width, barely affording footing for the horses, and midway a great rock had slipped down from above, resting on the narrow ledge by which we had to pass. This completely barred the way, and the perpendicular cliffs rendered it impossible for us to evade it by taking any other route. We therefore cut down a number of young pine trees, and using them as levers, set to work to dislodge the obstacle. After an hour's toil, we succeeded in loosening it from its position, and with a single bound it rolled down with sullen plunge into the deep river, far below. We then led the horses past, one by one, with the greatest caution. The path was so narrow and dangerous, that we gave it the name of Mahomet's Bridge.

The scenery at this point was very fine; the mountains shutting in the valley very closely on either side, and the river tearing and roaring along over its rocky bed with great velocity . . . A few hours' travelling in the morning of the 14th brought us to the Grand Fork of the Fraser, where an important branch from the north or north-east flows by five separate mouths into the main body of the Fraser . . . The situation is grand and striking beyond description. At bottom of a narrow rocky gorge, whose sides were clothed with dark pines, or, higher still, with light green shrubs, the boiling, impetuous Fraser dashed along. On every side the snowy heads of mighty hills crowded round, whilst, immediately behind us a giant of giants and immeasurably supreme, rose Robson's Peak. This magnificent mountain is of conical form, glacier-clothed and rugged. When we first caught sight of it, a cloud of mist partially enveloped the summit, but this presently rolled away, and we saw its upper portion dimmed by a necklace of light feathery clouds, beyond which its pointed apex of ice, glittering in the morning sun, shot up far into the blue heaven above, to a height of probably 10,000 to 15,000 feet. It was a glorious sight, and one that the Shuswaps of The Cache assured us had rarely been seen by human eyes, the summit being generally hidden by clouds.

. . . In the evening we arrived at The Cache [Tête Jaune Cache], and saw the bark slants of the Shuswaps [Natives] on the opposite side of the river; but waited till next morning before attempting to cross.

. . . We reached Tête Jaune Cache on the 17th of July, and on the morning of the 18th were ferried across the Fraser by the Indians. The water rolled over the bed of boulders at a great pace, swelling into large waves, on which the light dugouts of the Shuswaps tossed like a nutshell.

The foregoing story shows some of the difficulties faced by these adventurers, surveyors and railway builders, and it should be little surprise that so many lives were sacrificed in their endeavours. The railway only measured success in miles of completed track, and the order of the day was hard work by men who worked up to twelve-hour shifts for the sum of two or three dollars a day depending on capabilities.

During the summer of 1911, a tote road was completed from Mile 27, with tugs and scows moving supplies across Moose Lake to Tête Jaune. From there, courageous men loaded the supplies on scows and floated down the perilous Fraser River to forward camps, or on to Fort George. Slides and washouts were commonplace along the new grade and the thousand teams of horses working through the Yellowhead Pass during the winter of 1911–1912 were put to the test in trying to haul all the supplies to the forward camps. During the summer of 1913 there were twenty-four steam shovels and thousands of men working on the grade. Between injuries on the job and typhoid fever in the hospitals, life was often of short duration. The many graves along the right-of-way and in the hospital cemeteries testify to the fact that the medical staff often fought losing battles.

Prince George pioneer Carl Strom recalls his youth in the Willow River area and testifies that there were many graves in the hospital graveyard at Hospital Creek. As well, many other pioneers recalled the many unmarked graves along the right-of-way during their youth. One rumour persisted that a cemetery at Mile 29 near Red Pass contained several hundred graves.

The hospitals were located at Lucerne—Mile 3, Red Pass—Mile 27, Tête Jaune—Mile 53, McBride—Mile 90, Goat River—Mile 114, Dome Creek—Mile 146, Penny—Mile 163 (three miles west of Penny), Hutton—Mile 179, Eaglet Lake—Mile 207 and Willow River—Mile 217 (Hospital Creek near Willow River.) As well there was a hospital at the Cache in Fort George and another built on a scow that was moved along the river to wherever it was most needed. Many of these hospitals were little more than shacks, some of which were in use for a year or less.

It was a major task to keep food on hand for the enormous appetites of the hard-working men. Pat Burns' meat boat plied the river during the summer but it was impossible to keep the camps supplied. Hunters were hired to bring in whatever the woods offered in the way of wildlife. One of the hunters, Ernest Jensen, told me that moose and caribou didn't last long in the camps and bear meat was considered a delicacy. This was attested to by the area game warden when interviewed by a reporter from the *Herald*:

Several bears were killed in the camps around Mile 92 and bear meat was in general use at all the camps in that neighbourhood. At one camp, six bears were killed last month. It is earnestly desired that some of the meat would float down below the canyon. The men on the station camps are kicking against salt bacon and ham. "When? Oh, when is the fresh meat boat coming?" is the burden of their cry. That, and "For the love of Mike, send us a potato or we'll all have scurvy."

People were coming to the Fort George area by water or land, and some had strange tales to tell. J. Laurie and C.H. Cooke arrived from Saskatoon in March 1911 after an odd adventure. They had purchased tickets on the GTP Railway at Edson, their destination a town called Resplendent. When they arrived at the end-of-steel they learned that there was no such town. Finally they realized that the few stores, log cabins and tents was the town, and "Resplendent" was a portable town that just kept on moving with the end-of-steel.

GTP hunters at Dome Creek, 1913. Pioneer trapper and guide Ernest Jensen, third from left. COURTESY ARNA JENSEN

Imagine their surprise when they learned some time later that there really was a town called Resplendent farther down the line, and that they had paid fare for many more miles of train ride than they had enjoyed. The two men walked a considerable portion of the way to Fort George and took note that there were a thousand teams of horses freighting through the Yellowhead Pass.

As the GTP Railway neared the BC border, trouble along the right-of-way was anticipated, as suggested by an article in the *Herald* dated July 15, 1911:

> When Bill Miner held up a CPR [Canadian Pacific Railway] train at Ducks some seven years ago and made a getaway with a lot of coin and CPR bonds, the enormous rewards offered for his capture by the CPR and the government led every detective agency in the country to detail men to the chase. A party of the Northwest Mounted Police (NMP) obtained permission from the Federal authorities to join in the man-hunt, and they participated in his capture. A wrangle then arose between the NMP and the other authorities connected with the capture, as to the dispensation of the reward. This terminated in the relations between the provincial police and the mounted constables becoming strained for all time. From Tête Jaune Cache a report has recently reached us to the

A typical railway construction camp along the GTP Railway. Courtesy Prince George Railway Museum

effect that assistance to a man with a broken leg was refused by the mounted police until he was brought to their side of the provincial boundary. We hardly credit this, yet we know that in the Yellowhead Pass today the mounted police are keeping strictly on the Alberta side. The provincial authorities are now organizing the district around the Yellowhead Pass, where the construction gangs, with their inevitable lawless element are commencing to invade the Interior. It is being brought under the control of the provincial police, by the appointment of Mr. John Kirkup as administrator.

The foresight of the authorities was right on the money, as the incoming hordes brought bootleggers and criminals of all sorts. When Mr. A.K. Bouchier was justice of the peace at Tête Jaune during 1912, he sent an average of ten people a week to Kamloops on bootlegging charges. Many of those convicted got six months in jail. One bootlegger was picked up with ninety bottles of booze in his suitcases; the judge didn't believe it was for his own consumption so he levied a three-hundred-dollar fine. Another time a large shipment of booze arrived in the carcasses of hogs destined for the camp tables. One can't help but wonder if the cooks were involved.

An example of what was faced in that area was the murder of Big Julia, the largest man on railway construction. The December 7, 1912, edition of the *Herald* noted:

> What is said to be a feud of long standing over a woman resulted in the slaying of a man known along the GTP grade as "Big Julia," the strongest and biggest man on the grade. He was shot early last week by Frank Taft, a barber at Mile 29, BC.
>
> Taft, it appears, fired one shot from a .38 calibre revolver, at the labourer's heart. The bullet failed to take effect, and as "Big Julia" turned and ran, Taft fired at the abdomen, killing the man instantly. Only one man was an eyewitness to the affair.

Almost immediately after the shooting, Taft was taken into custody by Constable Campbell Nelson who, at the man's request, chartered a locomotive to take him to old Tête Jaune at Mile 50. Taft feared the men at Mile 29 would lynch him because of their apparent dislike for him.

Frank Taft, whose real name was James Munro Teaff, went to trial in Kamloops in May 1913. According to the *Herald*:

> The trial at Kamloops on the 15th, of James Munro Teaff, who was charged with murder at Tête Jaune Cache in November, resulted in an acquittal. The evidence showed that Julius Landree, the man Teaff is accused of murdering, was a man of Herculean build, who had treated other men with great violence and had broken the jaw of one witness. Teaff declared he had shot in self-defence. When the foreman of the jury announced that a verdict of not guilty had been reached, there was a burst of applause in the courtroom. Chief Justice Hunter stated that he agreed with the finding of the jury.

There is something rather difficult to grasp about the acquittal. One cannot help but wonder how Mr. Teaff managed to arouse such animosity among his peers that he was afraid of being lynched. Also questionable is his reason for shooting Julius in the back after he turned to leave. Most surprising of all, though, is the fact that neither Teaff nor Big Julia were known to indulge in intoxicants.

At the same time as this trial was progressing, Attorney General Bowser dismissed a special constable named Speed for fatally shooting a man named Magnuson at the Cache. The coroner's jury exonerated Speed but Chief Constable Bates held that the shooting was unjustified. The attorney general agreed.

In order to give some idea what the police had to contend with around these construction camps, it would be fitting to quote some passages from W. Lacey May's book *The Railroad and Current Mechanics*:

> Yellowhead Pass was put on the map of Canada only a few moons ago. Yet all through these mountain fastnesses lie the wrecks of villages that would in civilization have had their mayors and their social distinctions. But they never had mayors; they never had even the law that makes mayors, and

their inhabitants knew no distinctions for the simple reason that most of them were equally undesirable. The little groups of shacks that stand with empty doorways and the mere skeletons of roofs beside the new railway could not boast even of names in their most palmful days. The necessities of location were amply filled by the mileage along the railway grade—just as everything else is designated where steel precedes civilization.

"Mile 29" would convey nothing to the uninitiated, but to the bohunk [derogatory term for immigrants from central or southeast Europe] of construction it pictured a six months' career of revelry and dissipation. "Mile 50, BC," while specifically a spot 50 miles west of the summit of the pass, the boundary between Alberta and British Columbia, really meant a collection of log shacks that housed a number of "bad citizens."

It wasn't worthwhile to think of a name. They weren't there long enough to pay for the trouble. The "end-of-steel" villages they were called, and the term explained their existence. Wherever the "Pioneer"—the mechanical tracklayer that pushed the steel ahead of itself—lay up after overtaking the grade gang, there sprang up one of these villages. "The Pioneer"—an ungainly, dirty, overgrown boxcar, with the

Steam shovels did a great deal of work along the new grade. Courtesy Prince George Railway Museum

weird semi-human arms—never made a friend that clung so closely to it as did the end-of-steel village.

For where the Pioneer lies resting, hundreds of men are anchored within a mile or two, at work on ballast until the grade ahead is ready for another spurt of the track-layer. And only a few miles farther on, a portion of the grade-gang offers a weekend patronage that is not to be ignored by the village—the parasite of construction.

When the Pioneer decides to work for another few weeks every eye in the village watches for its next resting place, and when the first information comes a flitting takes place—an impromptu affair that is distinguished only by its simplicity and speed. There is no regret for a deserted home, only a careless ripping off of canvas roofs, a piling on flatcars or tote-wagons of the necessaries of trade, and a scurry for the choice locations of the new site. A day's work completes the place and the paraphernalia of the end-of-steel village is ready for operation without inconvenience to its patrons.

There is no indecision as to the location of the village once the end-of-steel is known. Just three miles away it settles down. That three miles is positively the only restraint it knows; for within that distance of the end of steel the contractor has complete legal control in unsettled districts. And, knowing the hell that lives in those shacks, he pushes them to the extreme of his authority. Within easy reach after his day's work, the bored, hungry bohunk, with money but no luxuries, no entertainment, no other means of expenditure, finds at the village every excitement and dissipation even he can desire. An end-of-steel village is made up of booze, billiards and belles. It is the home of the illicit liquor traffic of construction, the location of enough pool tables to stock a large city, and the residence of women who never elsewhere enjoyed so much freedom.

Three-quarters of the shacks are restaurants in front—for about six feet. On a short counter appear—uncovered except by flies—sandwiches, pies and cold meats. A patron of the restaurant alone is no more popular with the proprietors than is the restaurant with the average frequenter. The restaurant is merely an outward, plausible excuse for the existence of the shack. Back of the little counter is the poolroom—perhaps a score of tables that are only a shade less respectable and infinitely more a surprise than a restaurant. And then, through a small doorway, up a short flight of steps that breathe exclusiveness and privacy, is the real object of existence—the card room, where cards are but the means to an end.

Liquor knows no limits of location in the shack. You can buy it in the restaurant if you can't wait to go on farther. It is at your elbow between cue-strokes. The card-room reeks with it. That room puts the finishing touches on the bohunk that has passed from the front door through the several stages of poison. The bohunk that escapes the card-room with any satisfaction to himself has a petrified interior, and is a better manipulator of cards than the experts, or was able to draw first.

Pay bunk-houses exist precariously against the competition of their free brethren. The free bunkhouse is a provision of the contractors for the disabled, helpless bohunk that has spent the evening and everything else in the other shacks. A glance in one of them would carry conviction that the bohunk that patronizes them must be very, very helpless.

Police barracks at Mile 29, BC, c. 1911. Courtesy Violet Baxter

At Mile 50, BC, there was even a bath-house, but it failed ignominiously, but not unexpectedly. And at Mile 79 there was a constable's quarters—meaning a place where he could find protection from the weather and lend to things an appearance of law and order. In the daytime an end-of-steel village is respectable. There may be a little repairing to do after last night's carousal, but beyond that the only evidence of life is in the store signs. The tradesmen—and every one is that—concocts the wording of the sign and figures out the spelling. Most of his figures are more expressive than correct. And the only quality of art required is that the sign must be big and striking.

One big "general store" with a main sign that had evidently seen the hand of a professional, had accessory notices that within were cider, shooting gallery, a restaurant, and the repairing of shoes. That was a respectable sample. Education in an end-of-steel village does not run to letters. At night the place comes to life, for then its victims are free to offer themselves. The poor bohunk is just aching to clear the dust from his throat and to limber his body. In the village he finds everything from faro to frocks, pie to poison, dancing to death. In the lure of the first of the couplets he is thrust into the last.

If the open swindles of the camp fail to clean him out, the men who make a living there have few compunctions against "rolling" or even murder. The life of the bohunk is in the hands of his hosts, and they yield it to him only when his pockets are empty. An end-of-steel business has but one end in view, with few distinctions between fair and foul means.

In the Yellowhead Pass there were a half-dozen of these villages, with a dozen suburbs that sprang up where some exigency of conditions, such as a ford, congregated men or demanded a resting-place. At Fitzhugh [Jasper], Alberta, the lid was kept closed a little by the mounted police, but their jurisdiction ended at the border of BC, and there, at the summit, right on the boundary, the doors were opened wide, and down through Mile 17 and 29 and 50 they remained that way.

Mile 29 had a reputation which even its inhabitants refused to be proud. Situated in the heart of a difficult part of construction, it had an extended life that grew wilder with age. A special collection of shacks grew up at the western edge of the pass, on the site of the Tête Jaune Indian village, where the Grand Trunk Pacific emerged into the valley between the Rockies and the Selkirks. An old coloured woman ran the town, and she possessed all the qualities of a publicity commissioner. One of her weekend dances was warranted to drive boredom from the bohunk for a week—and often did more. An end-of-steel village is a disgrace, but Tête Jaune was indescribable. The only thing endurable about the settlements is their impermanence, but all the value of permanence is given by their wonderful powers of resurrection.

In fairness to the many people involved in running these cafés, rooming houses and poolrooms, it must be said that it was a means of earning a livelihood. Some of the people involved in these businesses went on to become solid citizens when opportunity presented itself.

The do-gooders didn't see it that way, though, so in an effort to counteract the terrible influence of the end-of-steel camps, several religions sent in missionaries. Called "skypilots," these men were faced with an enormous challenge. A spokesman for the mission noted, "It is the unique mission of the CCM (Columbia Coast Mission) to checkmate the grave evil of lonely camp life. When men are segregated by fifties and hundreds, often at great distances from civilization, such as on the transcontinental from Edmonton to Fort George, there is naturally a deadening effect upon the minds caused by the absence of diversified interests; the results in the majority of cases is a peculiar predisposition to the allurements of drink, immorality, gambling and other forms of vice."

Just how much success these missionaries achieved is questionable, as the end-of-steel shacks followed the Pioneer to the completion of the railroad.

To look at the problems and delays from the contractors' point of view, we need only read an excerpt from the *Herald* of August 23, 1913:

> ... The sub-contractors complain that although there is no difficulty in getting men, yet they cannot get the men they want, although they offer high prices for the services of such men. That the foreigners with whom they have to be content, are green, inexperienced, cannot speak any other language but their own and that they have to be taught their work from the very commencement. And then when they know a little they move on and a fresh batch of ignoramuses have to be taught all over again.
>
> One cause of delays—probably affecting all classes of labourers on construction, from the labourer (station men and day men) skilled mechanics, and the sub-contractors themselves, is dissatisfaction at the lack of good food supply. Complete lack in many camps of adequate medical attention and medical supplies, even the cheapest necessary aids to health and sanitation in camp life being wanting. The men are docked, each and every one, one dollar per month for this attendance and because they do not get it, even the ignorant foreigner from Europe, who is learning and learning more than his work and the language of his teachers, expects this and has a right to be dissatisfied if he does not get it.

As well, there were many complaints by the contractors that they were unable to get the rails and other supplies when needed, at times forcing them to feed their men for sitting idle. Many of the problems that faced the engineers along the grade were almost overwhelming. Many slides kept filling in the cuts that had been made at great expense. For instance, in July 1913 a huge slide dropped sixty thousand tons of earth, which completely filled in the cut. This slide occurred four miles west of Dome Creek in an area plagued by continuous slides. By some miracle only two men were injured and none killed.

Another slide at Knapp and Maloney's camp just west of Fort George had a different outcome. A man named Kostadin Angeloff was running a steam shovel when the hillside collapsed upon him, killing him instantly.

As the grade neared Fort George another accident occurred at Sam Magoffin's camp just east of the town. A small locomotive called a dinky engine was moving dump cars along the grade when the grade collapsed. The dump cars and engine were swept away by the river, but the crew survived.

No amount of peril or hardship could stop the railway's advance, with the result that January 27, 1914, was indeed a momentous day. At least 1,500 people lined up from the bridge to the railway station site in Fort George, and the continuous sound of applause greeted the tracklaying machine Pioneer as it entered the townsite. Though it was one of the coldest days of the year, nothing could prevent the people from showing their appreciation. The *Herald* wrote:

> . . . Among the distinctive features of the gathering, which was intended to symbolize the history and growth of the district, was a five-dog team belonging to Green Bros. and Burden—land surveyors. The toboggan was loaded with a typical surveyor's outfit, while a party accompanied it, with field instruments, axes, chains, etc.
>
> The Hudson's Bay Company, the pioneer of pioneers in this district, as well as elsewhere in the Canadian west, had its own proper representation—a company of trappers, dressed in toque and *ceinture flèche* [a brightly coloured sash worn around the waist by voyageurs] of the *habitant*, impersonated the early day adventurers who traded through this country for the great company.
>
> In spite of the extremely cold weather a brass band of ten pieces was on hand and played a number of selections although the musicians were compelled to edge up to an open fire to keep from freezing.

During the afternoon C.W. Moore, one of the 1907 pioneers, told the gathered crowd:

This day marks the end of pioneering in the Fort George country. For uncounted ages this has been the home of the moose, the bear, the beaver and the rabbit; and of the Indian, whose scanty living depended upon his skill in trapping and hunting them—pieced out by his patience and luck in fishing the salmon that came up the rivers to spawn.

The modern magician, the railroad engineer, has spoken his magic word and we now see the locomotive and the rails of steel. The joint creation of the last century, and without which modern civilization as we know it today, would not be possible. We are more than thankful in our welcome of the railroad and the men who built it. We believe in this place or we wouldn't be here; we believe it will grow rapidly into the most important inland city of BC. Many of us have staked our last dollar upon its future. It remains to us to make our investments win out and we can do it. We need do but one thing—that is to work united for the upbringing of our district.

There can be no doubt that the arrival of steel was by far the greatest day in the history of Prince George. One old-timer hit the

Tracklayer Pioneer crossing the temporary bridge to Fort George, January 27, 1914. COURTESY PRINCE GEORGE PUBLIC LIBRARY

nail right on the head when he observed, "The day that the railroad hit Prince George was the day that the feeling of isolation left here for good."

The day following the arrival of steel, ice jammed at the mouth of the Nechako, backing the water up and flooding the area of the Cache. Then the ice jammed up against the temporary bridge, causing four of the pile supports to give way. Another twenty-five were moved out of position, causing serious structural damage to the bridge. A family named Davidson—who operated a laundry in the Cache—became trapped by the high water along with their several children and were unable to cross the slough. Some hearty volunteers waded out and carried them to dry land. The man and woman were both badly chilled as they were in water up to their waists for a considerable period of time.

The railroad was completed in 1914, but at an enormous cost. The huge toll of human lives it took will never be fully known. One of the worst disasters along the grade occurred fifteen miles west of Tête Jaune, in an area that had been a constant source of slides because it contained a greasy sort of quicksand. A steam-shovel gang was working the area when a tremendous slide occurred, throwing the shovel and several men high into the air and into the river. A. McKinley, M. Munro and F. Ewe were killed in the accident and three other men

Ice damage to the temporary bridge, January 28, 1914. NORTHERN BC ARCHIVES AND SPECIAL COLLECTIONS, PARKER BONNEY COLLECTION, ACCESSION #2003.13.2

injured. A fourth man named J. Corpeck was seriously injured and taken to hospital in Edmonton. The volume of earth that descended in the slide was sufficient to block the Fraser River for a time.

Once the railroad was completed and in operation, three entrepreneurs decided to go into business at the railroad's expense. They began selling fake tickets and undercutting the carrier's price. It wasn't long before the men were hauled into court before Judge Taylor, who sentenced W. Holmes and G. Garow to four months at Fort Saskatchewan. The other man, A. Birchall, received a suspended sentence.

The excitement of the arrival of the railroad at Fort George quickly died down when people realized that they were not going to get instant and dependable service, as shown in the story of pioneer May Graham.

May met and married Bill Graham in Vancouver in 1908, and several years later they followed a wave of pioneers heading to Fort George. Bill and his brother Levi arrived first and were followed by their wives about a month later. From Edmonton, the women made it as far as McBride, BC, where they ran into delay after delay. From McBride to Fort George—a distance of less than 150 miles (241 km)—it took four more days, the train spending as much time off the rails as on them. Though the passengers had brought extra food with them in case of delays, they were unprepared for a trip of that duration. Travelling with them on the train was Fort George Sheriff Ernie Peters, and he took it upon himself to break into the locked boxcar containing food for P. Burns Store in Fort George. Here they found a vast array of foodstuffs, with which May and her sister-in-law did the cooking to provide the necessary nourishment for the passengers and train crew until they arrived in Fort George. This was during the winter of 1913–14, when an icejam destroyed portions of the temporary bridge across the Fraser River, so the weary travellers ended their journey by being ferried across the river in a boat.

Many large railway stations were built along the railroad grade, but in most cases people didn't settle near the stations, but rather around the sawmills. Many of these stations sat in isolation for years before they were moved to where the action was or were torn down. In a place called Guilford, about eighty miles (128 km) east of Prince

George, a huge station was built, which sat idle for about fifty years before it was destroyed. Except for a small cedar mill that operated for a couple of years, the only inhabitant was a fellow called Goofy Mike. Five miles distant was the mill site of Penny, which was served by a small station for many years. Five miles west of Penny another big station was erected at Lindup, a town with only a few inhabitants. Five miles to the west of Lindup was Longworth, another sawmill community with a tiny station.

Perhaps it would be unjust not to mention what many consider the greatest achievement of the GTP Railway—the Prince George Bridge. Since it was the crowning jewel of the western portion of the GTP, some statistics follow that may be of interest to the reader. This bridge is 2,658 feet and 10 inches between parapet walls. The clearance between the bottom chord and high water is about eleven feet and to low water about thirty feet. The lift span can be raised about forty feet, giving a clearance above high water of at least fifty feet and about seventy-five feet at ordinary water levels. The loading figured for the railroad track is composed of a train headed by two 180-ton locomotives, followed by cars giving a reaction of 4,750 pounds per lineal foot.

The extreme depth of excavation was thirty-five feet below water level. The cement plant, supplies, most of the materials and the men were transported in scows from the end of track down the Fraser River to the site, a distance varying from 150 to 195 miles. The bulk of the concrete was placed during extreme winter weather. The excavation started on August 21, 1913, and the bridge was finished on May 20, 1914. The superstructure was started April 1, 1914, and was finished January 5, 1915. There are about fourteen thousand cubic yards of concrete in the structure, and fifty-seven hundred tons of steel in the superstructure. The cost of the bridge was $1.6 million (about $80 million in today's currency).

It is worth mentioning that Johnson's Island (Goat Island) then stretched some distance above this bridge and was many times its present size; in fact, one of the piers was placed right through the island, which has since washed away from the area of the pier.

As soon as navigation opened for the 1914 season, a portion of the temporary bridge had to be removed to allow the steamers

Operator, Conveyor and *Hammond* access to the downriver markets. Some sources say that the lift span of the new steel bridge was only used once. This is not true. In fact, after the steamers *Operator* and *Conveyor* were pulled from service they were moved back through the bridge to the Cache, which was their final resting place.

Though there were a great many powder blasts along the railroad during the period 1908 to 1913, one of the biggest blasts occurred at a place called Point of Rock just west of Willow River, about twenty-five kilometres east of Prince George. This was one of the original FW&S caches, where a rock cliff stretched down to the river's edge. In preparation for the blast, the *Fort George Weekly Tribune* carried this article in the September 13, 1913, edition:

> It is stated by railroad men that 500,000 pounds of powder have been put into the rock hill that is to be blown up. Many scow loads of explosives have been brought down the river for this purpose. The big shot has been looked forward to eagerly by a number of people of this district, and several parties are planning to go up or near Mile 220 to watch the spectacle. Supt. Fetter, of FW&S will be there. He states that the safest point from which to watch the blast will be about two miles

The reaction ferry installed at Fort George during 1910 was still in use in 1915. Note the new GTP bridge and Johnson's Island in the distance. Courtesy Prince George Public Library

away. The Willow River Hospital commands a good view of the scene. Yesterday a small blast was set off at the point, preparatory to the main event.

In total three hundred tons of powder was exploded there at a cost of over $90,000 ($4.5 million).

Engineers on hand said it was the most successful piece of work that they had ever witnessed. A specialist was brought in from the coast, and he earned his pay with a perfect blast. Very little sound was heard, as all the energy went into moving the rock. Several months had been spent in digging the coyote holes to contain the explosives, during which time several lives were lost. Another two weeks were spent in filling the coyote holes with the powder. It was a momentous occasion and many people came to watch. The *Herald* noted:

> The blast was fired in two sections: the lower end, or about a third of the whole charge, being exploded late last week, and the balance of the shot was put off last Tuesday. The first shot [100 tons] did splendid work, breaking up the hill at the southern end, and wasting into the river only about sufficient yardage to leave the broken material easy to handle.
>
> The explosion of the main blast [200 tons] was an impressive sight. The big hill, at the turn of a switch, was seen to burst asunder in a huge volume of smoke, which shot outward across the face of the Fraser River and upward in great masses toward the sky.

When the smoke and dust cleared, there was the new grade! So precise was the blast that the Cache, only ninety metres distant, remained untouched by flying rock. The resulting broken rock was used as riprap for many miles along the river edge.

Before I make too much out of the powder blast at Point of Rock, though, perhaps I should mention that it pales in comparison to the blasting that went on along the Skeena Estuary for the GTP Railway. As hard as it is to believe, a total of fifty thousand tons of explosives were used in that area.

With fifteen hundred people in attendance, the GTP Railway was finally completed on April 6, 1914, when the last spike was driven two miles east of Fort Fraser, by Edson Chamberlain. As for the cost of the British Columbia section of the railroad, it was staggering to say the least. The estimate had been $80 million, but because of cost-plus contracts, which one contractor described as "nice to come home to," the final figure was $120 million. This would equal about $6 billion today.

The movement of supplies had been their most formidable challenge. At sixty pounds per yard, the weight of the steel rails between the BC–Alberta Boundary and Fort George totalled over twenty-four thousand tons, most of it having been moved downriver on scows or steamers. Also, the weight of concrete that was moved downriver for the construction of bridges and culverts was staggering to say the least.

The total distance from Winnipeg to the port of Prince Rupert was 1757.9 miles (2,813 km). All told, this railway was a bold undertaking and a great achievement without which the interior of BC would have remained in a state of isolation.

The accompanying picture of slides eight miles east of Penny, BC shows how supplies were moved from the railroad down to the river

Slides used for lowering supplies down to the Fraser River. COURTESY DON BARRY

for transport to camps on the opposite side of the river. One slide was for fuel and the other for food. The task of moving supplies across the river was eased somewhat by these slides.

Giscome Portage

A journey of sixty-five kilometres up the Fraser River from Prince George brings one to the Huble Homestead, a magnificent reminder of another era when it was stationed at Giscome Portage, the main access route through to the Peace River. Because Giscome Portage was such an integral part of the movement of men and supplies through the interior of BC, a brief summary of its history is in order.

The first record of non-Native use of the portage was in 1862, when a black prospector named John Giscome came north with a friend named Henry McDame (McDame Creek). Their intended destination was Fort St. James, but by the time they reached Fort George the Nechako River had frozen over. This forced them to overwinter in Fort George. Acting on advice from the Natives, they attempted to take the Salmon River route through to Fort McLeod in late April 1863. The river was too high and wild, so they abandoned that idea and followed their Native guide along a trail to the lake at the summit, which the local Natives called "Lhedesti," which means "the shortcut." They succeeded, and the rest is history. This explains why the portage still bears Giscome's name.

In the ensuing years many prospectors crossed to the Omineca goldfields and eventually petitioned the government to construct a wagon road across the seven-mile distance of the portage. In 1871 the government took action by hiring a man named John Trutch to corduroy a road from the Fraser River to Summit Lake. Following is an edited portion of a report written by Mr. Trutch while so employed:

Construction of Giscome Portage Road
Victoria, BC
August 25, 1871

Sir,
In submitting the following report of the wagon road across the Giscome Portage, connecting the Fraser River with the waters which flow northward to the Arctic Ocean, and with the construction of which I had the honor of being entrusted, I would refer you to my letter of April 5th, for particulars of my journey and reconnaissance from Quesnelmouth [present-day Quesnel] to the furthest point I reached north of Summit Lake.

On May 7th, I wrote to you again advising you of my proceedings up to that date, and informing you that I proposed to commence work on the road the following day, the necessary tools and provisions having just arrived. Accordingly the next morning I started the work with three men, the party being increased to twelve men during the course of the week. I had estimated that with a force of from forty to fifty men I should be able to complete the road in five or six weeks; and had accordingly procured tools for that number; but, after the arrival of the fleet of boats and canoes in the beginning of May, all travel by that route ceased, and I was never able to collect more than 21 men: the general average strength of the party being about 15 or 16. Finding there was but little probability of obtaining a larger number of white men, I sent down to Quesnelmouth, and endeavoured to engage some Chinamen; offering to give them $50 per month, and to pay their passage up; but after entertaining the proposition for a fortnight, they sent word that they would not come. The smallness of the party, and my utter powerlessness to increase its strength, caused me much chagrin and disappointment, as I had hoped, after completing the road, to be able to go on to Germansen Creek and return by the end of July. It was with great difficulty also that I was able to keep any men at work, as they were most restless and anxious to push on to the mines; and it was only their inability to obtain provisions and supplies that forced them to remain. The work consequently was carried on under great discouragement, and the attendant expenses were necessarily greater than they would have been had I been in a position to complete the road as originally contemplated.

Having been for five weeks without any news I started for Quesnelmouth on the 1st July, in the hope of getting letters, but more particularly for the purpose of obtaining funds to pay some of the men who were anxious to leave for Omineca; and on my way down the river received letters and telegrams directing me to repair as soon as possible to Victoria.

This I was unable to do until I had returned to the Portage, which I used all possible haste to accomplish; but the river still being very high, having fallen only four or five feet below high water mark, I did not succeed in getting back until the afternoon of Tuesday, 18th July. During this journey up the river of 13 days, we were on more than one occasion in the canoe for 14 hours, pulling ourselves along for two or three miles at a time by the overhanging branches of trees, the water being too deep for poling and too rapid to paddle against. We laboured under a great disadvantage also in having a canoe, which was heavy and ill suited to ascend such a swift river. Had I had a light Sower-river canoe I could have made the trip up in nine days.

The entire length of the road when completed will be seven miles and twenty-four chains [12 km], which is a little under the estimate seven and one-half miles I had formed of the distance. On the other hand there is considerably more

corduroying and more bridging and culverts than I had supposed would be necessary; much of the ground, after the snow
melted off, proving to be wet and swampy . . .

The first six miles from the river might be considered as
completed on the evening of the day I left the Portage; and
of this distance the portion between the river and the Three-
Mile Creek is constructed of a width of twelve feet. Fearing
that I should not have command of sufficient labour to complete the road, I reduced this width to ten feet, with turnouts
from the creek onwards. The grades are easy throughout, and
the road is thoroughly constructed, there being considerable
ditching and numerous culverts; but I fear that the first five
miles will be somewhat wet and muddy in the spring, as the
soil is for the most part composed of clay. This difficulty
will not be experienced in the portion next the lake, where
the ground is gravelly and sandy. At three miles from Fraser
River a bridge crosses a considerable stream one hundred
feet in length, the ordinary width of the stream being about
thirty feet. There are altogether five bridges, the aggregate
length being two hundred and fifty feet. The corduroying

Loading up to cross the Giscome Portage, c. 1912. COURTESY VIOLET BAXTER

and cross layering will amount to two thousand and fifty one feet, and there will be thirty-seven culverts . . .

John Trutch's letter gives us an appreciation of what he had to contend with. For example, the trying trip from Quesnellemouth up to Giscome Portage totalled 134 miles (214 km) against the powerful river current in an exceptionally heavy canoe and they completed the trip in thirteen gruelling days, averaging just over ten miles per day.

As it turned out, the movement through the portage in the 1860s and 1870s was just a warm-up for what was to come, because a man named Twelve-foot Davis was about to arrive on the scene. I quote the *Herald* of January 21, 1911:

> Years ago there lived and worked on the Fraser River, between Quesnel and Giscome Portage, a born transportation man. This man was Twelve-foot Davis. He derived this name in the Williams Creek [Barkerville] diggings through having discovered and staked a twelve-foot fraction that ran $1,000 to the foot. Today, amongst us at Fort George, may be noticed an old, bent Indian, whiskered and decent looking, and who by every moral right should be chief of his tribe, and would be, did he long for worldly honours. This was Twelve-foot Davis' right-hand man whom he trusted for years to steer his boats in perilous places. Probably a man who knows more about steering with a sweep or paddle than any living man on the mighty Peace and Fraser Rivers and their tributaries. An old Hudson's Bay Co. *engage* and trapper from time immemorial, with the honour of that honourable company deep in his soul, he is regarded by men of the north who know him, as a white man and the greatest judge of swift water imaginable.
>
> During the unrest in the Northwest and Manitoba during the Riel rebellion the Hudson's Bay Co. shipped flour to Vermillion and other Lower Peace River posts from Victoria; thence up the Fraser River to Quesnel by steamer, pack horses and freight teams. From Quesnel Twelve-foot Davis took the contract to land the freight at the lower Peace River posts. To this end three boats were constructed with a capacity of

15,000 pounds each, towed and manned by both Lillooet Indians and those of the Upper Fraser and Nechako. Three trips a season were made for three years to Giscome Portage.

During the autumn of each year 45,000 pounds were portaged on Indian backs and horses across to Summit Lake from the landing of Giscome annually. Three scows were constructed at the lake, carrying 15,000 pounds each, and five horses distributed on them for use at Rocky Mountain Canyon, Peace River, which is impassable. Here the scows were abandoned, and the cargo packed around the canyon, a distance of 15 miles to rafts below, on which the rest of the long journey was completed. On Davis' last season on this contract he built the largest boat ever hauled by men on the river, carrying 36,000 pounds, and the other three carrying 25,000 pounds each. Davis started from Quesnel with this cargo of flour in the spring. At Fort George he picked up 15 canoes for lightening purposes [moving freight through shallow water]. On arrival at Giscome Portage he hauled these large boats, as well as the cargoes, across the portage with the aid of four horses and his Indians. Only a fortnight was taken to accomplish this. An Indian's load of flour was 150 pounds, and he went half the distance of the portage without a rest. However, it was difficult to keep the boys from carrying more, as they wished to outdo one another. Reloading and after crossing Summit Lake it was discovered that there was not sufficient water to carry the large boat. Davis, never at a loss, lightened her up with his 15 canoes and built an immense dam, letting the water back up over night. In the morning the dam was quickly broken and the flood carried Davis and his fleet into deep water again and so on down the Crooked River into McLeods Lake, thence into the Pack River, where two more scows were constructed and the canoes abandoned. From the Pack the scows were taken into the Parsnip, thence into the Peace, through the dangerous Findlay and Pack Pass Rapids and on into Rocky Mountain Canyon—through which no boat can pass—and line her through and over the portage road to rafts below. The three smaller boats were brought back onto the Fraser River, but the largest one, with a sack of flour in its stern was sent intentionally to destruction through the canyon.

No reason was given for sending the big boat through the canyon, but probably all involved got a kick out of watching it being torn to pieces.

Throughout the 1880s H.F. "Twelve-foot" Davis and his crews did an enormous amount of work along the Crooked River, moving boulders and logjams to allow for easier transportation. Twelve-foot Davis was truly one of the great adventurers of his time. In retrospect it seems rather odd that the portage was not named after this outstanding individual, as he was the first person to use it for commercial purposes. Some sources suggest that Davie Lake was named after Davis, and I like to believe that is the case.

All told, Davis travelled the Portage and Crooked River for almost twenty years. After a lifetime of giving of himself, he died penniless and was laid to rest seven hundred feet above the town of Peace River. Thanks to the effort of his good friend Colonel Jim Cornwall, a monument was raised that states, "He was pathfinder, pioneer, miner and trader. He was every man's friend and never locked his cabin door."

There is no doubt that a great number of people used the portage throughout the early years, such as E. Barnum, who passed through the area and spent several days camped beside the Hudson's Bay post in the year 1895. He was on a prospecting trip to the Peace River area at the time and declared that Fort George was but a port-of-call for occasional, adventurous wanderers when he first saw it.

After Twelve-foot Davis left the Giscome Portage I was unable to find evidence of any other traders until A.G. Hamilton decided to operate a trading post at the site. Though his arrival date in the area remains cloudy, it appears that he opened his post about 1902 and either closed it or sold it a few years later. In 1906 he moved to Fort George and opened a store on District Lot 934 to run competition to the Hudson's Bay post.

Without question the most noted individuals to make a business of moving people and supplies through the portage to and from

Summit Lake were Edward A. Seebach and Albert James Huble. These two men met in Fort George in 1903 and struck up a friendship that lasted throughout their lives. In 1904 they started a business venture at the portage. Though I searched the records, I was unable to determine whether they took over the store, or trading post as these establishments were often referred to, from A.G. Hamilton, or built a new one.

Seebach and Huble were competent woodsmen; they were fur traders, trappers, farmers and merchants. Their trading post at the Giscome Portage was capable of supplying travellers to and from the northern rivers with almost all necessities. As well, these two traders even made a few dollars by supplying firewood for the voracious appetites of the sternwheelers, which often loaded five cords of firewood at a time. Cutting firewood was a winter project that brought additional revenue to many along the waterway. They also found time to improve the trail across the portage and spent many years moving equipment and supplies with horses and a Red River cart.

An example of what they had to contend with while living in such a remote area was given in the following story carried in the *Herald* on January 28, 1911:

> Giscome Portage is an interesting, historical point. It is 41 miles north of South Fort George, on the Fraser River. It is one of the avenues into the Omineca country . . . Some 27 settlers have located there, and all are apparently satisfied with their pre-emptions. There is a store there conducted by Seebach and Huble, which has been in existence for five years. The 27 pre-emptors have been agitating for a post office and some means for getting mail at least once in six months. The present arrangements are as primitive as man can find. They have not had mail since January of last year, and in order to forward letters to the nearest post office, which is in South Fort George, the pre-emptors assemble at a given point on a set day, and draw lots to see who will be the lucky man to break a 41-mile trail with snowshoes from Giscome to South Fort George. The short straw this year fell to Ed Seebach, possibly because he has more correspondence than any other individual man at that point. A strange coincidence, how-

ever, is that the same man has broken the trail for four con-
secutive years, and he feels doubly sore at being a Dominion
servant without a salary. On one of these trips Ed had both
feet frozen, and today carries evidence of what pioneer work
is in the north. With all the handicaps in his way, Ed Seebach
came down in two days.

Giscome Portage advertisement in the *Herald*, September 1914.

Despite their isolation, it was a rare election day when they did not take the long walk to South Fort George to register their votes. Even thirty-below-zero weather did not deter them. The *Fort George Tribune* noted in 1909:

> Ed Seebach and A.J. Huble of Giscome Portage, 41 miles up the Fraser River from Fort George, came in to vote. The coldest it had been was eight below zero, but there was about four feet of snow. They returned this morning.

During the summer of 1911, two adventurous souls made their way from Edmonton to the headwaters of the Fraser River. Their mission was to run the river to Giscome Portage and then return to Edmonton by way of the Peace River. After a trying trip down the river, they portaged the upper portion of the Grand Canyon and, after careful scrutiny, ran the lower section in their collapsible canoe, which they called the *Blunderbuss*.

In his book, *New Rivers of the North*, Hulbert Footner described the elation they experienced while running the lower canyon. After a few more days on the river they arrived at the Portage, where the author noted:

> After several false discoveries Giscombe Portage finally stole into view around a bend. We had been told that there was nothing to mark the place but a couple of Chinamen's shacks that we might easily miss; however, we found that civilization had now reached a tentacle up the river. A store has been erected on the bank along with two or three little dwellings with gardens at their sides. There were not less than a dozen souls about the place, giving us after our lonely voyage quite the effect of a metropolis.
>
> Of the dozen, five were hardy young adventurers who had preceeded us down the river on a raft. They had a tale to tell of the whirlpools in the second canyon, which had nearly put a period to their journey. When we modestly confessed to having run it, they looked at the *Blunderbuss* and smiled politely. They were bound for Fort George down the river, the Mecca of the real estate agents.

... It transpired that the storekeepers at Giscome kept a team [of horses] for the purpose of transporting outfits across the portage. They were outrageous brigands, the pair of them, and even now my choler rises hotly at the recollection of the twenty cents a pound they forced us to pay for sugar and the dollar and a half for a tin of cocoa that we coveted. Ten dollars was asked to carry our sixty-pound boat and two hundred pounds of baggage for six miles. As they carried a three-hundred-pound bell at the same time, we compromised at seven ...

I couldn't help but chuckle at the complaints of the author. Perhaps it never occurred to him that there would not have been service across the portage if these two men had been unable to make a living there. There must have been precious little activity to derive income from during the winter months, except for the occasional trapper using the portage.

The suggestion that they were "outrageous brigands" was out of line, as I have found no reason to believe that a fortune was made during their many years of hard work in the portage area. In fact, giving credit where it is deserved, the Huble Homestead was given to the present-day heritage society by the Huble family.

Seebach and Huble moving supplies at Giscome Portage. NORTHERN BC ARCHIVES AND SPECIAL COLLECTIONS, PARKER BONNEY COLLECTION

Both Albert Huble (often misspelled Hubble) and Ed Seebach were constantly in the news. The *Herald* of June 20, 1914 noted:

> Mr. Seebach of Giscome Portage was in town this week on business. The above firm runs the motorboat *Giscombe* from H.P. Spur Mile 194, BC [Upper Fraser on the GTP Railway] every Wednesday to Summit Lake, and can arrange for transportation to any point in the Parsnip, Finlay and Peace River District. Mr. Seebach reports there are a large number [of people] going up into the Peace this year and that he is in a position to make contracts for taking any amount of freight at reasonable rates into this country.

The moving of their pickup point to Mile 194, just west of Upper Fraser, meant that they now had access to the new railroad, which was to supply them with clientele from east and west. As well, they had the traffic from north and south, as they were still served by the steamer *Quesnel* from Prince George in 1915. This steamer made frequent trips to the Mile 194 spur line dock on the river, where goods were transferred from rail to boat and vice versa.

GISCOMBE PORTAGE TO SUMMIT LAKE

It is the intention of this firm to start a freight service from Giscombe to Summit Lake this month. Outfits will be transferred to any point on the route. Parties who intend going into that country this coming season can be assured of the best service possible. Goods forwarded c/o Haynes and Wood, Giscombe Portage, will be stored until the arrival of owner.

Haynes and Wood

Haynes and Wood advertisement taken from the *Herald*, September 19, 1914.

Early in 1914 two other men moved to the portage and competed with Seebach and Huble. As far as I can determine they were the only other people to attempt to make a living moving supplies through the Giscome Portage. "Shorty" Haynes and Les Wood were to advertise for only a year before they gave up and Shorty moved on.

The *Herald* of April 11, 1914, carried the following notice:

> Emmet Haynes, who, with his partner Mr. Wood, is start- ing in the business of transporting supplies from Giscombe Portage to Summit Lake on the Peace River water route, is in town today making preparations for the season's business. "Shorty" Haynes, as he is familiarly known, is a well-known old-timer in this district and has a knowledge of the upper country and the vagaries of river navigation possessed by few. Incidentally, it might be mentioned that "Shorty" is some inches over six feet in height.

Much admired by his peers, Emmet Baxter "Shorty" Haynes was a huge and powerful individual who was involved in the disappear- ance of fellow trapper William Allan Goodson along the Torpy River during the late winter of 1926. A decorated soldier during the First World War where he was employed as a sniper, Shorty travelled the Fraser River constantly throughout the years 1909 to 1930. His name will live on in the area of the portage, as nearby Emmet Creek was named after this memorable pioneer.

The picture on the following page, taken along the Torpy River about 1930, shows Shorty Haynes on the left and fellow trapper Carl Swanson at centre. Take note of the dogs in the picture, because dogs were an integral part of the lives of these pioneer trappers. The cabin in the picture eventually tumbled into the river when the bank washed away.

Prior to the railway construction, Giscome Portage was served by the steamers during the summer months, but with the arrival of the rail- way, it became such a hassle for the steamers to get through the GTP bridge—what with having to lift the span—that freight movement to the Giscome Portage by steamer was no longer feasible. The steamer *Quesnel* made a few trips in 1915 before giving up the venture.

Apparently the GTP Railway did not want to cooperate in lifting the bridge span, at times suggesting that a train was coming and the track had to be clear. Several times no trains showed up for hours, and the steamer owners finally threw up their hands in despair and gave up. This is probably the reason Seebach and Huble moved their location for pickup of supplies to the GTP spur line at Mile 194, just west of Upper Fraser. Known as Hudson's Bay Spur—because the Hudson's Bay Company used it in their shipments to the North—this new dispatch point meant that Seebach and Huble were no longer forced to haul all of their supplies upriver to the portage by motorboat or steamer. Rather, they were at a distinct advantage because they were moving freight downriver to the portage instead of against the current from Prince George.

One would think that the usefulness of the Giscome Portage ended in October 1919 when a road was completed between Prince George and Summit Lake, but that was not the case. The firm of Seebach and Huble continued their business of moving people

Shorty Haynes, Carl Swanson and an unknown man at Shorty's cabin on the Torpy River, c. 1930. Courtesy Jim Chambers

and supplies through the portage, as shown by the advertisement below.

The following item carried in the *Prince George Citizen* dated November 3, 1922, provided proof that Seebach and Huble were also fur traders:

> Thomas Van Dyke, provincial game warden, made a haul at Summit Lake last Friday night, while on patrol. He was awakened late in the night by the sound of an approaching boat and was down at the landing when it came in. The craft was in charge of E.A. Seebach of the trading firm of Seebach and Huble, and the cargo consisted of 50 beaver skins and a quantity of rats, minks, weasels and marten. The skins were promptly seized and Seebach was charged with being unlawfully in possession of them, as the season had not yet opened. He appeared before Magistrate Herne on Tuesday and was fined $200 and costs. The skins, valued at $600 to $700, were confiscated.

After Seebach and Huble moved from the Portage area, their former competitor Les Wood leased the property. In 1927 a rich American woman named Josephine Mitchell bought the property in partnership with Les Wood and renamed it the W.M. Ranch. A man

Seebach and Huble advertisement taken from the *Prince George Citizen* of July 30, 1920.

named Ivan Wayant was also involved. Their dream was to build a dude ranch, but the venture fell through and Mrs. Mitchell bought out the other two men and went on to build a large ranch on the land. Ivan Wayant stayed on as her ranch foreman.

Long after the Huble family moved from the area, large amounts of freight were still moved through the Crooked River. During the summer of 1923 the federal government employed men to remove many of the rocks impeding traffic along the waterway. As late as 1927 three hundred tons of freight was moved along this river.

However, road construction eventually spelled an end to the use-fulness of the portage. As for Seebach and Huble, their names will rightfully live on in the area, because two streams bear their names in the forests east of the portage, along the traplines they travelled for many years. As well, the Giscome Portage should and will live on in the history of the Interior because it has been restored and is now known as the Huble Homestead/Giscome Portage Historic Site. It has become a favourite tourist spot and is visited by a great number of people each year.

The Huble Homestead/Giscome Portage Historical Society has done an outstanding job of restoring the original Huble buildings and it is worthwhile for anyone to spend at least a day there. The por-tage trail has been rebuilt and is an enjoyable and scenic walk. A day at the homestead can truly roll back the years and cause one to ap-preciate the sacrifices made by these pioneers. The Giscome Portage played an integral part in the development of the Interior, and was as necessary in its time for providing assistance to travellers to and from the northern waterways as the GTP Railway was in providing this same assistance between east and west in later years.

Since it has not been my intent to deal with events along the rivers north of the Giscome Portage, I must suggest that people who are interested in the movement of people and supplies along the Crooked, Pack, Findlay and Peace Rivers should read *Crooked River Rats* by Bernard McKay. It gives a detailed account of freighting along those waterways until much of the area was submerged beneath Williston Lake.

A final point I must make about the waters north of the Giscome Portage concerns boats. While the freighters on those waters were using the Corless riverboat design, the riverboats in general use on the upper Fraser River were tubs by comparison. Trapper, guide and riverman Oliver Prather was the first person to adopt the Corless design to the Fraser and it was an instant success. Oliver told me that he first saw the design in use at Summit Lake and was so impressed that he took all the measurements and promptly built one. The rest, as they say, is history.

Now I want to shift gears and bring in a story about a place called Caribou Meadows or Caribou Basin, seventy kilometres east of Prince George. This area is in the mountains south of the Grand Canyon, which is now part of the Sugarbowl–Grizzly Den Provincial Park. While discussing the anecdotal evidence that the Natives used to hunt caribou in the area of the meadows, it was pointed out to me that the hunting of caribou in that area must have taken place only since the Natives acquired rifles. This is not necessarily the case, and one only has to read history books to understand this. The Natives definitely hunted big game long before they acquired rifles. One of the techniques they used was to build a fence, perhaps in a valley high in the mountains. Spaces were left between some of the fence-posts with snares hanging from them. With great care the hunters would surround the caribou and then drive them toward the fence.

The Huble Homestead as it appears today. COURTESY OF GISCOME PORTAGE/HUBLE HOMESTEAD HISTORICAL SOCIETY

Other hunters and even young boys were stationed along the sides of the valley to prevent the animals from escaping in those directions. When the animals reached the fence, they naturally went between the posts, where the snares awaited them. Some of the animals would pick up the snares, pull the posts out of the ground and run only a short distance before they became tangled in the trees or brush. Then the hunters rushed quickly in among them to prevent them from escaping the snares.

The old saying that "necessity is the mother of invention" was certainly proven true by the Natives, and why not? Their very existence depended on their creativity. It must be understood that these hunts in Caribou Basin were enormous undertakings, as their supply-laden canoes had to be paddled 160 kilometres upriver from their homes in Fort George prior to the hunt. Next was an uphill journey of about fifteen kilometres. After the game was secured, all the meat and hides had to be carried back to the bottom of the Grand Canyon, where their canoes awaited them. Then they still had the 160-kilometre return trip to deal with. No easy task, but what an astounding adventure it must have been for the boys and young men!

In these days of supermarket shopping, it is difficult for us to appreciate the importance of collecting food for even the barest of existences, something the Native people understood only too well. It brings back memories of my childhood, memories of my mother putting the garden away for the winter. There were hundreds of sealers full of canned vegetables and fruits and a cellar crammed with fresh vegetables such as onions, potatoes, carrots, beets, turnips and cabbages. It was truly a special feeling at that time of year to know that there was enough food put away to last the entire winter. Sometimes a huge harvest moon would shine down, perhaps checking to see that all was well.

After the Steamers

Travellers continued to follow the river after railway construction, and fortunately some of them left a record of their adventures. During the summer of 1936 an adventurous Scotsman named Edgar Reid decided to follow in the footsteps of the early explorers. In his book *Fast Flows the Fraser*, Edgar details his trip from Tête Jaune to Big Bar Creek on the lower Fraser, a distance of over five hundred miles (800 km).

On the second day into his trip he wrote, "What a soul-stirring feeling it is to be alone on the Great River, alone with the great power that I can feel surging beneath me as I am swept swiftly along on its flood waters [1936 was the year of the great flood on the upper Fraser]. Eventually I know—if I can but tag along—this great force will take me through mountain gorges to the sea. Can I, just an ordinary kind of guy, hope to go along with the million-horsepower potential in all its unharnessed fury and survive? I don't know, but I am all for rushing in and having a go at it."

Edgar's main concern was the Grand Canyon about which he had read and heard many horrifying stories. At every opportunity he questioned prospectors or stump ranchers that lived along the waterway. Many told him to consult a bush foreman named Jake Smedley, affectionately known to his peers as "Big Ugly Jake." Jake had been one of the Canyon Cats during railway construction, so he was the proper man to talk to. Edgar followed directions and found the camp farther down the river. This is how he described his meeting with Jake:

> From what this experienced riverman tells me it is no uncommon occurrence for one of the Grand Canyon whirlpools to up-end a 200-foot Douglas fir tree, take it for a merry-go-round and then suck it out of sight. The mighty tree, I am told, might never be seen again in its entirety, only fragments of it appearing again downstream. "Matchwood, my boy," says Jake.

Disregarding Jake's warning, Edgar tackled the canyon in his rubberized canoe. On July 25 he wrote:

> I expect something pretty bad from all the stories I have heard about this Grand Canyon and believe me I am certainly not disappointed in what I see before me . . . From a normal width of about 200 yards, the mighty river is suddenly bottled between 50 feet of rock. Through this narrow opening the great volume of water surges in great, rolling waves, bounding with energy. Like a racehorse at the barrier fretting for action, I muse. Carefully putting away my camera, with which I had hoped to get some good pictures of the canyon's entrance, I firmly grip my double-bladed paddle and brace myself for what I now realize is indeed a desperate venture.
>
> Suddenly, with a rush and a roar the rolling waves break into raging rapids. Down a 75-yard straightaway I tear to make almost a right-angled turn into equally boiling waters around a rocky bend in the river. With pent-up fury as though rebelling at the delay, the wild waters make the most of a gradual descent to gain an even greater momentum before turning once more to dash out of the upper canyon into what seems, by comparison, to be a peaceful lake.

Here the suddenly becalmed waters rest for a moment, and so does a rather dazed canoeist, but not for long. I soon discover that my "lake" is in reality a dam. This, I soon find, leads into a smaller canyon, complete with its full quota of rocks, rapids and some of the hungriest, sucking whirlpools seen in my whole 500-mile Fraser River journey.

With a quick glance to see if my surf sheet is still in place, I decide to chance the rapids rather than flirt with the whimsies of the whirlpools and the rocks. These I know have wrecked many a craft during railway construction days between Tête Jaune Cache and Prince George.

I have but a second to make my choice. The die is cast. For better or for worse, here I am entering the lower waters of the Grand Canyon with all its roar and turmoil.

Can you imagine a giant water main suddenly bursting in a thousand places, releasing tons of water in all directions? If you can, then perhaps you have some idea what it was like inside that canyon on the upper Fraser as the glacial waters hurled themselves pell-mell between the rocky ramparts.

Battling it out with the rapids in midstream, the first thing I know I am caught in a crossfire action of raging waters. Suddenly out of nowhere it seems, a wave ups and strikes me on the chest with a blow like a sledgehammer. Luckily I have the presence of mind to bring up my knees from under the surf sheet to trough off the water that is threatening at any moment to swamp the canoe. This instinctive act of self-preservation undoubtedly is the only thing that saved me from being swept under and away by the raging torrent.

What happened to me during my run through that "roaring rapid" is better left between myself and my Creator who saw fit to bring me through right side up. When you look death face to face it certainly gives you plenty to think about and you suddenly find out how big or how small you are. Let it suffice that when I gain the welcome calm waters that usually prevail at the lower end of canyons, I know all my failings as a canoeist at least, and I am equally well aware, and thankful, that a Power much greater than my own has been with me all the way.

Suddenly I perk up as I remember with gratitude, the kindly, understanding offer of Jake Smedley, the riverman, who knew the Grand Canyon, and knowing it had tried to persuade me to keep out of it. "If you get through the canyon, better pull into my cabin at the lower end. Get some food into you and get dried out," had been his last words as I said goodbye to him the day before. The preposition used may have been "when," but at that moment I thought it was "if".

Edgar Reid survived his hazardous journey through the canyon, but his writings make it plain that he pushed his luck to the limit. In later years he summed up his feelings by writing:

In the yawning, hungry depths of a whirlpool one day I felt the clammy breath of death. For one long moment as my up-ended canoe was about to be pulled out of sight, I thought that my number had come up—this time for sure. As I paddled desperately to keep from being sucked under by the relentless power of the mighty whirlpool, suddenly a miracle happened. The good Lord reached out and plucked me from a watery grave. More dead than alive, I managed to paddle my water-filled canoe to shore and safety . . . Many times in my dreams I am still confronted with rushing rapids, or great sucking whirlpools that keep reaching out suddenly to pull me under fast-flowing waters. I have only to turn the pages of my old daily journal and it all springs to life again—that desperate, youthful plan of mine to follow in Simon Fraser's footsteps along the wild river that bears his name.

Pioneer trapper and guide Glen Hooker of Dome Creek, BC, recalled a special memory from the 1930s. This concerned a log chute that protruded down off the high cutbanks a few miles upriver of Dome Creek. Logs were placed into this chute, where they came downhill at an incredible speed to a bench, where the chute ended. From that point the logs were in free fall until they struck the water of the Fraser River with a resounding splash. When one of these airborne logs hit another log coming down from upriver, pieces of wood were seen flying all the way across the river. In low water, some of the bigger logs drove down into the river bottom where they had rocks from the river bottom driven into the wood. This required that the end of the log be sawn off before they could be cut in the mill. There is a story about a man named Frank Wagner, who was running upriver with his motor-boat when a log roared off the chute and passed just over his boat, right between him and a friend seated in the front. Thankfully no one was injured and no lives were lost delivering logs to the mighty Fraser River in this strange way.

All throughout the years between the 1920s and the late 1960s, area sawmills drove logs along the river as well as through the Grand Canyon. During those years there were many experienced rivermen involved in this work. Of all these riverman, it can be accurately stated that Ray Mueller was the person that travelled that area the most. As Ray lived about eight miles downriver from the

Ray Mueller and his son Don, on the right, break a mighty logjam in the Grand Canyon, 1966. Courtesy Louisa Mueller

canyon, he not only moved logs along the river, but also frequently travelled through the area as a trapper and guide. Sometimes referred to as "Mr. Canyon," Ray probably knew the turbulent monster as well as the Canyon Cats who worked the area many years earlier.

One of Ray's favourite stories concerned a job he worked on with several other men. During the course of their duties, he often had to move the others through the canyon in his riverboat. Sometimes these fellows would stand up in the riverboat, which really annoyed Ray. Many times he told them of the danger, but his warnings fell on deaf ears. On one trip he was moving along near where the whirlpool often displayed its might; this day it was quiet. With all hands standing up, the big eddy suddenly opened its yawning mouth and the entire crew found themselves staring down into the seething vortex. In one motion the entire crew sat down and Ray never had to issue another warning after that.

Another of Ray's stories was about a raft-load of about twenty Chinese that ventured into the canyon about 1911. The raft got pulled into the whirlpool and sucked under; all on board were lost. Torsten Berg of Prince George confirmed this story. Years ago Torsten was a friend of Jake Smedley, one of the Canyon Cats. Jake assured Torsten that these men had indeed been lost in the canyon.

Oliver Prather was another individual who travelled the canyon area for many years. Born in 1921 in the nearby community of Longworth, he first went to the canyon with his father about 1927, when the planked tramway between the warehouses was still plainly visible. As a young man, he worked in the logging camp where Jake Smedley was foreman. Oliver says that Jake and another Canyon Cat named Norman Scott both had cabins and homesteads right near the canyon. Oliver remembers that both cabins were still there during his youth.

When asked if he ever had any problems running the canyon, Oliver replied, "Only once, when I sheared a pin in the upper canyon, but I managed to get into the eddy near Green's Rock, where I changed the pin. That's the only time I got a scare there, but I always treated the area with respect because you never know what can happen."

Oliver's brother, Arnold Prather, also worked the canyon for many years, and he will not soon forget the close call he had in its wild water. This event took place during the mid-1950s when Arnold left Cornell Mills and headed upriver to pick up some timber cruisers at Driscoll Creek. Arnold was carrying a load of planks in the front end of his riverboat when he entered the upper canyon, and his boat must have been overloaded or front heavy, because the first wave that

Trapper and guide Oliver Prather in the Canadian Navy, c.1945. Courtesy Louisa Mueller

hit came over the top; the second wave filled the boat and caused it to roll over. Arnold's luck was with him that day, because he was wearing a life jacket. He hung onto the boat until it drifted against Cannibal Bar, and then he fastened two floating logs together. By this means he managed to get to shore.

The following day, Oliver got word that his brother Arnold had not arrived in the community of Longworth as expected. He headed upriver and feared for the worst when he found the overturned boat against the bar. A short time later his spirits were lifted when he found the flotation device on the door of a cabin where Arnold had spent the previous night. A few miles upriver he found Arnold walking along the riverbank, none the worse for his experience but harbouring a deep respect for the power of the river.

Bill Batten, who was the mill manager at Penny for several years, had his own showdown with the canyon. The year was 1956 and Bill was on his way through the canyon in a twelve-foot plywood boat when he struck a rock and sheared a pin. Helpless in the wild water, he managed to get the boat close to shore, where he jumped to safety. The boat drifted on through the canyon without overturning and in due course made its way into the Sinclair Mills booming ground thirteen kilometres downriver. Throughout the hours that the boat was drifting, Bill had a choice: stay put and hope someone came along, or walk the riverbank back to Penny, a distance of about twenty-five miles. He gambled on waiting, and after several hours had passed, along came Ray Mueller in his riverboat, towing Bill's boat, which had escaped the canyon undamaged. Bill's boat was just one of several that went through the canyon unattended, but not all the other boats fared as well as his.

Perhaps the old saying "familiarity breeds contempt" is true. At least it may seem that way when one hears Eric Klaubauf's story about the canyon. After running it successfully for several years, Eric didn't seem to be concerned about travelling it at any stage of water. But then there was the day . . .

In the summer of 1960, he and a companion named Richard Foisey went up into the canyon and were attempting to climb the upper rapids. On that particular trip, Eric was using a 40-foot riverboat that had previously been powered by a 75-horsepower motor, but on this occasion, he was using only a 40-horsepower engine. As they attempted to climb the upper rapids, the front of the boat went up on a wave and when the bow tipped down, the stern came out of the water and the boat stopped. As the boat went back into the trough, a wave came over the stern and dropped a load of water into the boat. For some reason Richard burst into laughter. Again Eric took a run at the same spot and again they slid back and took half a boatload of water. Richard stopped laughing at that point and grabbed an empty dynamite box with which he began bailing water as though his life depended on it, which it probably did. Realizing they were in trouble, Eric took the boat back into calm water, where they bailed the water out. Then all the supplies were moved to the back of the boat. This stopped the stern from coming out of the water and allowed them to get on through the upper rapids. They had flotation devices in the boat at the time, but they were of a very poor design, always dirty and usually wet. They would have been a liability rather than an asset, so the crew never wore them.

Eric has another story that is worth recording for posterity. It involves river driving, or in this case, creek driving logs. This story began in 1955 when a boxcar-load of dynamite arrived in Dome Creek in preparation for blasting log sweeps and rocks out of Slim Creek about 125 kilometres east of Prince George. Even small islands in the centre of the stream were blown to kingdom come that summer.

During the next three winters, decks of logs were piled high along the stream. When high water arrived in June, supports were pulled out from under the streamside of the decks, which allowed them to fall into the creek. This was almost farcical at times, as the logs jammed up against rocks or roots that protruded into the stream. The silence of the wilderness was frequently broken that summer by the charges of dynamite placed among these logjams. At times parts of logs were seen flying through the sky. Many returned to earth and stuck upright in the ground as if they had grown there.

Eric was one of the riverboat operators during the three years of these drives, and recalls that he had a few accidents around the rapids in the stream. One day they were attempting to climb the rapids when the pin in the propeller sheared. Pushed by the powerful current, the boat came back sideways against a large rock and folded up like an accordion when the two sides came together. The boat was repaired after a fashion, but it leaked water to such an extent that two people were needed at all times—one to run the motor and the other to bail out water with an empty dynamite box.

The other accident took place when a pin sheared and the boat came down against a sweep. The men climbed onto the tree just as the boat was swept under it and thereby prevented a possible tragedy.

Eric recalled when the river foreman, Buster Van de Reit, refused to let them use dynamite. He suggested they use a crosscut saw instead. After several hours of trying to cut off a log sweep in the powerful current, Buster gave up and went for a walk while Eric blew the sweep.

Eric told me that no one had a ticket to use dynamite, they just learned as they went along, and often used more powder than required. When I questioned the use of powder in a salmon stream, I was informed that Penny Spruce Mills was fined the sum of six hundred dollars after an area trapper reported the blasting. I found it most surprising that the men never found any dead fish floating along the stream after these blasts were set off. Perhaps the fish had all moved down into the river because of the powerful current during high water.

Looking back, it seems almost unbelievable that a boxcar-load of dynamite was used in a salmon stream, but such things happened. Surely a similar act today would result in a few years' imprisonment, but in those days it was "get the job done or someone else would."

It would be hard to picture a more deadly hazard than an unmarked cable spanning a river, hiding out of view just beneath the surface. This situation has arisen many times throughout the years and has resulted in fatalities as well as near-fatalities. One individual who struck a cable with a riverboat was lucky enough to live to tell the story, but only because he was a powerful swimmer. This accident took place in the spring of 1955, when Ian "Bruce" MacAskie was returning to Penny by riverboat after a day of cruising timber up Slim Creek for Penny Spruce Mills. This is his story:

I was approaching Moose Island on my way downriver when I decided to take the westerly channel. Things were going

well as I passed Joe Pastor's farm, but trouble came on fast
as I swung out of the side channel into the main stem of the
Fraser River. The 14-foot boat I was using had a long shaft
on the motor, which caught on something below the surface of the water. The sensation was an odd one, as if in slow
motion, and as the boat came to a complete stop, I noticed a
log-boom cable gradually lifting up from the water, obviously
connected to the riverbank on one side and to the island on
the other side.

At that point, the boat took the full force of the river over
the transom and I was immediately swimming for my life. The
swim itself would have been more tolerable had it not been
for the working equipment fastened around my waist. I carried a .38 cal. service revolver, which was a standard part of
my kit, as well as an Abney level, belt axe, increment bore,
field compass and a metal container that held my field notes.
To make matters even worse, I was wearing heavy clothing,
which included long underwear, wool mackinaw jacket and

Huge logjam in the Grand Canyon, 1956. The water rose five metres behind
the jam. COURTESY CHARLIE BENTON

high-top leather boots. Life jackets were not considered a requirement at that time.

The daylight was fading fast as I spilled out of the boat into the freezing river water and it was all I could do to get my bearings and start swimming toward the closest shore. I felt certain that the weight of the equipment and my heavy clothing were going to take me down. I swam on, and it seemed like a long time until my boots hit solid ground. When I got on the bank, I collapsed exhausted and was surprised to find that my briar pipe was clenched between my teeth and still lit.

By the time my strength returned, it was dark and I was forced to stumble through the forest and swamps until I spotted the lights of a house. The people [Joe and Mary Pastor] kindly invited me in and offered tea and comfort until I warmed up and was able to continue on my way. It was a miserable trek back to the comforts of home, but I considered myself lucky and was happy to be alive.

Bruce was indeed fortunate to have survived the river, but another cable incident proved much more deadly. This took place

Bruce MacAskie at Tumuch Lake, 1954. Jack Boudreau photo

during the summer of 1961, when a terrible accident happened at the Grand Canyon involving two timber cruisers, Ernie Pement and Sterla "Slim" Roe. During the course of their work cruising timber, Sterla had fractured an ankle, so they called for help. Pilot Bill Harvey answered the call and flew to their rescue in a Hiller 12E helicopter. Bill took the men aboard the helicopter and decided to show them the nearby Grand Canyon. While doing so, they flew right into an unmarked cable that spanned the river. The chopper crashed into the river, and after a brief struggle, all three men managed to get out of the aircraft. Slim was doing his best, swimming along with a broken ankle, while Ernie swam near him. Suddenly Ernie began crying for help. Perhaps because of an injury, he was unable to swim to shore and drifted into the lower canyon, where he drowned. At the same time Bill, who could not swim, was in serious trouble. Then a miracle happened—an empty ten-gallon drum that had been fastened to the outside carrying racks of the chopper broke free and popped up right beside him. Bill desperately clung to it and eventually made it to shore some distance farther down the river. Slim had already made it to safety and was in the process of searching for his partner, who had already drowned.

And so it appears that Ernie Pement was the last person to drown in this rugged canyon. Let's hope that he will remain so, for it is certain that this canyon has already claimed too many lives.

In total, it has been estimated that this canyon has claimed up to two hundred lives. In his magnificent book *Sternwheel Days* Art Downs states that over fifty people were drowned in the Grand Canyon during 1913 alone.

Several sources state that fifteen hundred men piloted scows along the river in 1913, and that about ten percent of these scows were lost; most certainly a large number of these pilots were lost as well. When we add in the people that were lost from the countless hundreds who made their way through on rafts, dugout canoes and boats, it may be that the number exceeds two hundred. Whatever the final number, it is obvious that it was substantial.

Often the bodies of the drowned were never recovered. This may seem strange, but when one considers the enormous amount of steel, cable, cement and other material that was lost, then it is small wonder that many bodies did not resurface, but instead remained tangled in the debris below. As for the bodies that were recovered, many were buried in unmarked graves.

In regard to the infamous Green's Rock that destroyed so many scows, Frank Freeman blasted much of it out of existence. As well, Ray Mueller blasted part of the top off it in 1966 because it was continually causing logjams right in the worst part of the canyon. Why Frank Freeman never blasted more off Green's Rock is unknown; perhaps it was a case of priority and he dealt with the most pressing spots in the canyons and rapids along the 650 kilometres of the Fraser and Nechako Rivers placed in his care. It should also be noted that the two serious steamer accidents that occurred above Fort George took place before Frank Freeman blasted in those areas.

Frank Freeman continued on with his work of blasting the rapids and canyons. During the winter of 1913–14 he and a group of men spent several months blasting at Soda Creek Canyon in an effort to extend the range of the steamers for another fifty miles. The days of the steamers along the upper river were numbered, though, and Frank's legacy can best be remembered by a fitting tribute he received for his dangerous blasting work in the canyons and rapids along the river. It was printed in the *Herald* dated August 24, 1912, an edited portion of which follows:

THE RIVER HOG

There arrived in town this week from the upper river a big fair man in a green shirt that was rent by a flying rock up in the Grand Canyon. There he is driving a gang of rock men in his work of clearing the obstructions to navigation out of the river, and tearing out a steamboat channel with dynamite and steel. His name is F.C. Freeman, but among his familiar friends he passes muster under the name of the "River Hog." He is a silent person, this river hog, speaking only when you ask him things, and then not answering in any length. He works for the railway contractors FW&S, and his task is to free the river they want the great sternwheelers to navigate, from the rocks that threaten their safety on the river. A few weeks ago the SS *Operator*, a boat that can load 300 tons of freight, crashed on a rock in the Goat River Rapids and her crew jettisoned about 150 tons of freight in order to save her from total destruction. Since then the "River Hog" has visited the Goat Rapids with a crew of his men and a load of dynamite, and a clean channel has been blown in the living rock of the riverbed. No longer are the Goat Rapids a menace to navigation, or a place to whiten the hair of the river captains who gamble their skill against the rocks that lurk in ambush beneath the muddy waters of the great river that flows so swiftly on toward the sea.

In the Grand Canyon Freeman is tearing the land to pieces where it crowds the water too closely. From the riverbed, with steel and dynamite, under his direction, men are clawing the hungry rocks. The great walls of the Canyon give back roaring echoes as huge charges of powder in the coyote holes shatter the rocks, and the waters close quietly over the scar in the canyon's jaw.

The "River Hog" is now commencing operations up the Nechako River. The White Mud Rapids and the Isle de Pierre,

Frank Freeman is flanked by Josie and Frank Hinsberger in Penny, 1925.
COURTESY BESSIE BOUDREAU

both dangerous chutes of rock-strewn, white water, will be harnessed and broken, and made to run smoothly through a wide, deep channel.

. . . You might see him sometimes, if you travel the river these days. Probably seated upon some rock by a wicked piece of water, chewing tobacco and watching the race of the flood as he learns the secrets of the channel, by the waters that foam and eddy past. Determined from his knowledge of river lore, he will spit with precision into the torrent that roars about his resting place, a cynical smile upon his face.

And so we leave him to his task, this "River Hog." He has a big task in these northern waters, but he is used to handling big jobs. When he passes along there will be many a placid shoot of water where the river has lain in wait, with death at hand, to trap the unwary as they run the gauntlet.

Frank Freeman spent Christmas 1912 in Fort George. His presence was noted and appreciated by the *Herald* when it wrote:

His gangs have done huge execution in removing the rocks from the Fraser and Nechako Rivers, and through his work the steamboat trips will be safer but less exciting.

After his blasting days were finished, Frank Freeman spent a few years in the small community of Penny, where he became a close friend to my parents. Perhaps because of the stories I heard about this man from my parents in my youth, I have always held a place of deep respect for him in my heart.

Frank passed away in the Prince George Hospital in August 1931 following a bout with pneumonia. He was plagued during the last few years of his life with recurrent lung troubles, possibly brought on by staying too close to the powder blasts that were his trademark. A pioneer who gave much of himself, Frank will mainly be remembered for his dangerous work in the canyons and rapids that he helped tame.

People who travel through the Grand Canyon, as well as the

Giscome, White Mud, Isle de Pierre and Goat River Rapids in the future should take note that they are a far cry from what they were in 1911. Since that time, thanks to Frank Freeman and his blasting crew, all of the most dangerous rocks and boulders have been blown away.

Present-day people may wonder why so many people risked so much in the Grand Canyon and other danger spots along the river. Perhaps this was best answered by a man who survived the river when he stated, "We really didn't have much of a choice; we had to make a living somehow."

And so this mighty canyon still stands—sometimes peaceful, sometimes a raging monster—but to those who visit it, may it not be asking too much that they stand for a moment's silence in memory of the courageous people who perished there. Perhaps some day we will build a monument to all who were lost there and in the other rapids and canyons along the river, such as the one built at Jasper, Alberta, which is inscribed with the words:

THE OVERLANDERS OF 1862

Commemorating the courage and daring of the parties of gold-seekers, who in 1862, left their homes in Upper and Lower Canada and journeyed overland by way of Fort Garry and Edmonton to Kamloops and Cariboo, pioneering an immigrant road to British Columbia. The only organized overland immigration from Eastern to Western Canada prior to the era of railway.

At a traffic pullout on Highway 5 about sixty kilometres north of Kamloops, BC, another sign has been erected that reads:

OVERLANDERS OF 1862

It had been an epic struggle against the wilderness for the gold-seekers from Eastern Canada. They had crossed the Rockies, trekked through pathless forests, and won the swift rapids of the North Thompson River. The open country now offered hope and safe passage. Ragged and starved, they reached Kamloops where many became pioneer farmers.

If such a monument is ever erected along the Fraser River, it should also recognize the enormous loss of life during railway construction, and pay tribute to the Natives who risked and sacrificed their lives while supplying the many survey camps along the upper river. Such a monument would be our way of saying to all of them that we have not forgotten; that we will forever honour the sacrifices they made in the opening of this great province.

DISTANCES BETWEEN POINTS MENTIONED IN THIS BOOK

The following distances were taken from the *Fort George Herald*.

Fort George is central for a large area of country, the greater part of which is suitable for farming. It is located near the geographical centre of the province and at the junction of two rivers, which are navigable for steamboats for 675 miles (1,086 km). Going east and southeast, following the Fraser River upstream are the following points:

Distances from Fort George

	Miles	Km
Goose Country Ranch	16	26
Mouth of Little Salmon River	22	35
Mouth of Willow River	25	40
Giscome Portage	41	66
Mouth of Big Salmon (McGregor) River	68	109
Mouth of Bear (Bowron) River	81	130
Mouth of Tonequah (54) Creek	95	153
Head of Grand Canyon	106	171
Slim Creek	139	224
Dome Creek	156	251
Clearwater (Torpy) River	164	264
Smoky (Morkill) River	188	303
Goat River	204	328
Snowshoe Rapids	218	351
Moose Rapids	220	354
Beaver River	257	414
Shuswap (North Thompson) River	264	425

	Miles	Km
Tête Jaune Cache (head of navigation)	315	507
BC–Alberta Boundary	368	592

At Giscome Portage a wagon road of eight miles connects Fraser River with Summit Lake, which flows into the Parsnip River, also called the south fork of Peace River. The Findlay River is the north fork and from their junction the river is called the Peace, which eventually flows into the Arctic Ocean. The distances from Fort George via Giscome Portage are:

	Miles	Km
Summit Lake	49	79
Fort McLeod on McLeod Lake	116	187
Mouth of Parsnip River	196	316
Fort Grahame, on Findlay River	261	420
Ingenica Mines, on McConnell Creek	360	580
Fort St. John, on Peace River	360	580

Going west, northwest and upstream on the Nechako and Stewart (Stuart) Rivers:

	Miles	Km
Mud (Chilako—river of beaver) River	20	32
White Mud Rapids (Bar Rapids)	22	35
Upper White Mud Rapids (Sestino Rapids)	24	39
Isle de Pierre Rapids (Stone Rapids)	33	53
Wavy Rapids	35	56
Stuart River (Chinlac Rapids)	57	92
Stoney Creek		
(via Stoney Creek Trail 75 miles)	90	145
Fort Fraser		
(via Stoney Creek Trail 101 miles)	120	193
Fort St. James (via Stewart or Stuart River)	139	224
Burns Lake, on Telegraph Trail	156	251
Aldermere	237	381
Hazelton		
(head of navigation on the Skeena River)	297	478
Prince Rupert	459	739

Heading south downriver:

	Miles	Km
Indian or Hudson's Bay Gardens	5	8
Fort George Canyon	15	24
Hixon Creek Trail	45	72
China (Chinchula) Rapids	50	80
Blackwater River	60	97
Cottonwood Canyon	75	121
Quesnel	95	153
Soda Creek	155	250

SOURCES

Sources of information and corroboration regarding the Grand Canyon

BC Historical Quarterly (many issues).

Cariboo Observer, Quesnel, BC.

Downs, Art. Sternwheel Days.

Edmonton Journal, Edmonton, Alberta.

Edson-Jasper Signal, Jasper, Alberta.

Footner, Hulbert. New Rivers of the North.

Fort George Herald, Prince George, BC.

Fort George Tribune, Prince George, BC.

Fort George Weekly Tribune, Prince George, BC.

Hutchison, Bruce. The Fraser.

May, W. Lacey. The Railroad and Current Mechanics.

Milton, Viscount and Cheadle, Dr. W. The Northwest Passage by Land.

Morice, A.G. The History of the Northern Interior of British Columbia.

Ramsey, Bruce. John Giscome's Country.

Reid, Edgar. Fast Flows the Fraser.

Runnalls, Rev. F.E. A History of Prince George.

Talbot, Fred. The Making of a Great Canadian Railway.

——————. The New Garden of Canada.

Turner, J. Turner. Three Years Hunting and Trapping in America and the Great Northwest.

Wade, Mark. The Overlanders.

Walker, Russell R. Bacon, Beans 'n Brave Hearts.

Washburn, Stanley. Trails, Trappers and Tenderfeet.

Anecdotal sources of information (taken over many years)
Torsten Berg, Prince George, BC.
Ole Hansen, Prince George, BC.
Mrs. Kay Houghtaling, Prince George,BC.
Gus Lund, Prince George, BC.
Louisa and Ray Mueller, Sinclair Mills, BC.
Wayne Mueller, Sinclair Mills, BC.
Oliver Prather, Prince George, BC.
Elizabeth and Dale Sinclair, Prince George, BC.
Carl Strom, Prince George, BC.
Bill Tuckwood, Penny, BC.
Olive and Ted Williams, Prince George, BC.

Sources of Pictures
BC Archives, Victoria, BC.
Jean and Charlie Benton, Kamloops, BC.
Marion and Jim Chambers, Kamloops, BC.
Elarry Evasin, Prince George, BC.
Eric Klaubauf, Prince George, BC.
Elmer Micks, Terrace, BC.
Louisa Mueller, Sinclair Mills, BC.
Prince George River Boat Association, Prince George, BC.
Prince George Public Library, Prince George, BC.
School District #57 Heritage Collection, Craftsman
    Photographer.
Elizabeth and Dale Sinclair, Prince George, BC.
Fred Spurr, Prince George, BC.
University of Northern BC Archives, Prince George, BC.
Olive Williams, Prince George, BC.

Map designations
Bob Dondale, Prince George, BC.
Eric Klaubauf, Prince George, BC.
Wayne Mueller, Sinclair Mills, BC.
Mike Nash, Prince George, BC.
Oliver Prather, Prince George, BC.

INDEX